The
EVERYTHING®
Golf Instruction Book

Dear Reader:

Most golf books are written by the world's finest golfers who have long forgotten what it's like to shank half a dozen consecutive shots. However, this book is written by an ex-hacker who wakes up in a cold sweat every now and then from a dream about incurable slices and topped shots, and a golf coach who's seen the frustrations of scholarship athletes who have tons of talent, but scant ounces of patience. That's a long way to say we know your game.

We can help you learn the swing for the first time or put new keys in your brain to help you find that elusive swing that's just right for you. We can teach you how to take what a course gives and execute the surest shots to get out of trouble and avoid disaster.

Golf is the perfect blend of physical and mental challenges. Success comes not from perfect mastery of the game—all golfers are doomed to fail in such an attempt—but from taking pleasure in the pilgrimage, from straighter shots and better lag putts to improved distance control and wiser decisions.

You can do it, and we're glad to help.

The EVERYTHING® Series

Editorial

Publishing Director	Gary M. Krebs
Managing Editor	Kate McBride
Copy Chief	Laura MacLaughlin
Acquisitions Editor	Eric Hall
Development Editor	Lesley Bolton
Production Editor	Khrysti Nazzaro

Production

Production Director	Susan Beale
Production Manager	Michelle Roy Kelly
Series Designers	Daria Perreault
	Colleen Cunningham
Cover Design	Paul Beatrice
	Frank Rivera
Layout and Graphics	Colleen Cunningham
	Rachael Eiben
	Michelle Roy Kelly
	Daria Perreault
	Erin Ring
Series Cover Artist	Barry Littmann
Interior Illustrator	Kathie Kelleher

Visit the entire Everything® Series at everything.com

THE
EVERYTHING®
GOLF INSTRUCTION BOOK

From teeing off to sinking the putt,
all you need to play the game

Rob Blumer and Dr. Rex Chaney

Adams Media Corporation
Avon, Massachusetts

An Everything® Series Book.
Everything® is a registered trademark of Adams Media Corporation.

Published by Adams Media Corporation
57 Littlefield Street, Avon, MA 02322 U.S.A.
www.adamsmedia.com

ISBN: 1-58062-672-6
Printed in the United States of America.

J I H G F E D C B A

Library of Congress Cataloging-in-Publication Data
Blumer, Rob.
The everything golf instruction book / Rob Blumer and Rex Chaney.
p.   cm.   (An everything series book)
ISBN 1-58062-672-6
1. Golf. I. Chaney, Rex. II. Title. III. Series. Everything series.

GV965 .B5595 2003
796.353'3–dc21
                                            2002015051

This publication is designed to provide accurate and authoritative information with
regard to the subject matter covered. It is sold with the understanding that the publisher is not engaged in rendering legal, accounting, or other professional advice.
If legal advice or other expert assistance is required, the services of a competent
professional person should be sought.
        —From a *Declaration of Principles* jointly adopted by a Committee of the
American Bar Association and a Committee of Publishers and Associations

Many of the designations used by manufacturers and sellers to distinguish their
products are claimed as trademarks. Where those designations appear in this book
and Adams Media was aware of a trademark claim, the designations have been
printed with initial capital letters.

This book is available at quantity discounts for bulk purchases.
For information, call 1-800-872-5627.

Contents

THE
EVERYTHING®
GOLF INSTRUCTION BOOK

Top Ten Things You Will Learn
After Reading This Book

1. How to master the rules and etiquette of the game.
2. What equipment to buy and how to avoid breaking the bank.
3. Where to practice and which exercises will improve your game.
4. How to perfect your body positioning with proper stance, shoulder slant, and knee flex.
5. How to grip the club to ensure accuracy and power, and prevent injury.
6. How to focus on your target and visualize your shot.
7. How to coordinate all the parts of your body to ensure a fluid swing.
8. The physics of ball motion and the causes of hooks, slices, and pulls.
9. How to play from bunkers and avoid bad lies and hazards.
10. How to perfect your short game and putt like a pro.

Introduction

▶ THE GAME OF GOLF has been played for over 600 years. It was already being played on those hallowed grounds known as the Royal and Ancient Golf Course in St. Andrews by the time of the founding of the great St. Andrews University in Scotland in 1411. The clubs have changed from sticks of driftwood, to wooden shafts with wooden heads crafted by bow makers, to the hi-tech alloys of today's game. The balls have changed from leather pouches stuffed with feathers, to tightly wound wonders with titanium cores on the inside and computer-configured dimple patterns on the covers. Yet, the game is the same, and the passion of its players—hackers to tour pros—is as hot today as it was when Mary Queen of Scots played a round too soon after her husband's murder and was criticized for doing so.

Golf is a lifetime sport, and it's the only truly multigenerational sport. Play over the centuries has yielded ingenious rules that allow anyone who can swing a club to compete with anyone else of any age, and of any ability. An average Jane or Joe doesn't have a chance to experience the thrill of batting in the bottom of the ninth at Yankee Stadium, but there are numerous golf courses around the country and in Europe where the less than average golfing Joes and Janes can pit their skills against the very holes that once brought great golfers to ruin, or elevated their names to immortality.

Golf is a mysterious game. It's part science, part art, and part alchemy. You can find great teachers and gifted pros who differ over how to swing the club—what happens first, how the weight is balanced, and so on. There are hackers whose hacking is mystifying because their swings seem okay at a glance, and outstanding professionals whose swings shouldn't work as effectively as they do.

This book helps to unveil the mystery of the swing, although it can never strip the game of its mystique. You'll learn troubleshooting tips to help you diagnose and correct hooks, slices, topping, and hitting behind the ball. You'll find drills to make your swing more reliable and exercises to keep your game strong and youthful. And, you'll learn to match wits with the design of a golf course to help ensure that the great swing you're developing is properly applied with club selection and shot target to improve your scoring.

Keep in mind as you're reading that most golf courses are designed for right-handed players. Though this may not seem fair, it's one of those facts of life that you must come to accept. Therefore, this book is written with the right-handed golfer in mind. If you're left-handed, you may need to alter the instruction somewhat, in regards to mention of "right" and "left." However, for the most part, the authors have tried to guide you by referring to "front" (the side closest to the target) or "back" (the side farthest from the target) instead of the specific right or left.

The great American author Mark Twain called golf "a long walk, spoiled." Poor fellow. Perhaps he thought he should have been able to command a three iron as easily as he controlled his pen. You'll never master the game. No one has, ever. Not Tiger, or Jack, or Arnie. Not Ben Hogan, or Sam Snead, or Gene Sarazen, or Bobby Jones. So, toss aside your frustrations, look forward to the conundrums, and enjoy the journey. You're about to improve your game.

Chapter 1
Learning the Game

There are almost as many nuances to the rules of golf as there are obscure rules in the tax code. But don't worry, you don't need to know everything—or even a whole lot for that matter—to play golf. Your best bet is to get some of the basics down and then just get out there and play.

Golf Course Terminology

You're going to learn much more about the terminology and the decisions you need to make as you play the game. You can't possibly know everything at first. (You can't possibly know everything about golf—ever.) However, there are a few basic terms you need to know.

Too Many Tees?

The word "tee" is used as either of two nouns, or one verb. The first noun, "tee," is that little wooden stake used to "tee up" the ball for the first stroke on a given hole. A player doesn't need to use one, but most do, even on short par threes. The tee helps the player place the ball on a perfect lie even if the ball is practically at ground level.

The second noun, "tee," indicates the area of the course from which a given hole is begun. The actual term, a term you'll probably never hear (unless your playing partner is a Scotsman) is "teeing ground." You usually hear it referred to as "the tee" or the "tee box." Usually, it's a little mound of green space with tee markers and a sign indicating the length of the hole and the par for the hole.

The verb "to tee" means "to set the ball on a tee" or "to get started," as in "All right, let's tee it up."

QUESTION?

What does "lie" mean?
In golf, when we refer to "lie," we're talking about the position of the ball at rest. So, when we say the ball is on a perfect lie, we mean the ball came to rest at the perfect spot. "Lie" is less frequently used to refer to the angle formed by the shaft and the club head in relation to the ball.

Tee Markers

Tee markers are those objects of a given color, mounted close to the ground, that indicate the line beyond which a golf ball may not be "teed up" on a given hole. On most golf courses there are usually several sets of tee markers. On an eighteen-hole course, there will be a set of tee markers for the front nine, and another set of markers indicating the teeing ground for the back nine holes. This second set of markers changes the length of the hole and/or angle of the flight path the ball will take to the green. Usually, there are two sets of markers marking the women's teeing ground, too. On some golf courses that also host significant tournaments, there will be a set of championship tee markers, usually increasing the lengths of most of the holes by many yards.

Standing on the tee and looking toward the green, the ball must be teed between or behind the markers, though never more than two club lengths behind them. It's a one-stroke penalty to tee your ball further back. Since the markers can't be moved, a player will sometimes tee a ball very close to a tee marker, and stand so that the marker is between the ball and his or her stance. This is perfectly acceptable.

FACT

Never be afraid to leave the driver in your bag. Even on long holes, better control and less distance often improves your chances for a good score more than trying to boom the driver and sending the ball on a hike through the woods. Also, the stroke required for a good drive is different from the stroke used for all the other shots.

Terrain Terminology

On a par four or five, your shot off the tee (the teeing ground, the tee box) should ideally land in the fairway. On a par three, you plan for your tee shot to land on the green. The fairway is the well-manicured part of the long space between the teeing ground and the green. The grass is cut very short so that, far more often than not, when a tee shot rolls to a stop, the lie of the ball will be perfect—the ball won't be in a hole or snuggled up next to a clump of grass, but will be sitting on top of the grass—hence the "fair" (pleasant) way.

All the area on either side of the fairway is the rough. Some courses simply allow the grass to grow a bit taller along the sides of the fairway, calling that area the "intermediate rough." You'll also hear it called the "first cut" of rough. Beyond the intermediate rough is the rough: weeds, logs, thickets, you name it.

Beyond the rough is out-of-bounds. This term means just exactly what you would think. A ball that is out-of-bounds is out of play. On some golf courses, it's easy to tell on practically every hole where the out-of-bounds markers will be and what constitutes out-of-bounds. (Here's a hint: If the course you're playing is in a neighborhood, everyone's backyard is out-of-bounds, along with swimming pools and rear decks.) The rule for playing the next stroke after a ball goes out-of-bounds is to take a penalty stroke and play the next shot from "as nearly as possible at the spot from which the original ball was last played," according to the USGA's Rule 27-1.

It's often best in the deep rough to choose the prudent shot over the most heroic. Instead of aiming for the green through that narrow slot between a dozen trees, turn sideways (or even back toward the tee if necessary) and punch the ball out of trouble and onto the fairway.

Rules to Get You Going

The easiest way to understand the basic rules of golf is to play a hole. Don't try to memorize the rules and page numbers of the official United States Golf Association (USGA) Rules of Golf, just concentrate on getting from the tee to the hole. If you grew up playing football, basketball, soccer, baseball, or any other sport, think about how many rules you learned simply by playing the game—rules you would never realize you know unless you consult that sport's official handbook. So, let's tee it up and learn!

Teeing Off and Honors

Assume that you're being initiated to a round of golf by three friends who all play the game regularly. Everyone spreads out and swings a club to loosen up. Chances are, this round of golf is taking place on a weekend, meaning that another group of players will be teeing off a few minutes after your scheduled "tee time."

If your foursome is going to go strictly by the rules, somebody will flip a coin or draw straws to see who goes first. However, this rarely happens. On the first tee, someone usually says, "Okay, who's up?" If this is your first time playing, it's generally best to refrain from volunteering to go first. If you keep quiet, someone will tell you when to go. If there's a woman in the foursome, the guys will probably tee off first on the first hole, because the women's tees are closer to the green by a few to fifty yards, depending on the hole.

After the first hole, honors—being first to tee off—goes to the person with the lowest score on the previous hole. If two or more members of the foursome tie for honors, honors belongs to the one who had the lowest score on the hole completed prior to this last one.

The Mulligan

It's often understood in friendly rounds of golf that everyone gets a mulligan. A mulligan is a second chance, or a "do over," but it doesn't exist in the Rules of Golf, even though it's often the norm when playing with friends. Usually a mulligan is one extra shot from the tee, one time, if it's needed. Never assume that a new group you are playing with allows mulligans. Some more serious golfers, even serious bad golfers, don't consider them.

Stand on the opposite side of the ball from the person preparing to hit, and stand still. Never stand directly behind the ball and in line with the intended direction of the shot—it's illegal, even on the putting green.

Whiffs and Accidental Bumps

You've been to the driving range a few times to get ready for this first round of golf. The pressure mounts as you line up your first tee shot with eyes watching. You take a couple of practice swings, line up, and go for it. Whiff. The ball hasn't moved.

In a casual round of golf, probably no one will care, but it is supposed to count as a stroke. If you line up to hit the ball, make a swing, and miss, it's a stroke, unless you made an effort to stop your swing. On the other hand, if you set the driver behind the ball, and while lining up the shot, the club knocks the ball off the tee, it isn't a stroke. Why not? You weren't swinging, so tipping the ball off the tee doesn't count against you.

Out of Play

When you've actually made contact with the ball, the next thing to worry about is where it's going to land. It could land safely in the fairway, a fairway bunker, or in the rough. The ball could also land out of play—out-of-bounds or in a water hazard.

If you're a purist and a stickler for the rules, you know that a ball in the lake is not "out of play," technically speaking. However, a ball landing in a water hazard is unplayable most of the time, and you'll likely decide it's out of play. Of course, you can also decide to give your partners a good laugh, put on concrete golf shoes, descend into the deep, and try to hit it out.

Out-of-bounds balls are absolutely out of play, no matter how easily you can see the ball. The out-of-bounds markers might hug the edge of a fairway, be hidden deep in the woods, or border the fences of homes, pools, and gardens of people who have built along the fairways of the course you play.

Penalty Stroke

So what happens if you sent your ball for a bath or into someone's backyard? You have a choice. You can always play the next shot from "as nearly as possible at the spot from which the original ball was last played," meaning you can tee it up again if your ball went AWOL from the tee, or drop the ball near the spot on the course from which you launched that wayward shot.

Your other option is to walk toward the pond or the out-of-bounds markers along the line of flight taken by your ball, and take a drop along that line. This means you should hold out a ball at shoulder height and drop it to the ground along the line of flight, but never nearer to the hole than the line of flight. In the case of many water hazards, golf courses will often have a convenient drop zone. It's usually a good place from which to play the next shot.

You'll incur a penalty stroke for hitting a ball out-of-bounds, or determining that the ball in the water is unplayable. Assume, for example, the shot that went out-of-bounds was off the tee. Whether you hit from the tee a second time, or take a drop, your next shot will be your third, not your second.

ALERT!

Suppose your ball lands in a shallow creek. You could wade in and take a whack. But even the pros are usually better off taking a drop and the one-stroke penalty. However, if a tournament is on the line and a penalty stroke will take them out of contention, pros will roll up their trousers and take their chances.

First to Play Is the One Away

After the tee shot, the away ball—the ball farthest from the hole—is the ball that's hit first. If you're en route to your next shot and someone has stopped to prepare for a shot, be sure to stay way out of the way. Once that player has lined up the shot and addressed the ball, stop. Wait for that player to complete the shot and watch the ball's flight in case he or she needs help locating it, and then continue on toward your own ball.

Waving a Faster Group Through

If a ball from your group sails into the woods, it's always proper to help your playing partner to locate it. While you hunt for the errant shot, look back toward the tee (or on a long par five, look back to the fairway) to see if another group is waiting on you.

Let's say that when you approach the edge of the thicket, it becomes apparent that finding the ball is going to be work. Everyone plunges in to hunt, but in seconds, a member of your group motions to the pair of golfers standing on the first tee. Immediately, those two play their tee shots, then, after walking to their golf balls, they play their approach shots to the green.

At about the time they're lining up putts, your foursome finds the lost ball.

Instead of following through with the intention of placing that ball on the green and into the cup, your playing companion in the woods waits on the pair of golfers, now putting, to hole out (get the ball in the hole) and to vacate the green. After all, it simply isn't proper to shoot for the green when the players in the match in front of you are putting.

If your ball goes into the woods, first tell your playing partners that you're hitting a provisional ball. If you can't find the ball in the woods, you've saved time; take your penalty stroke and play the provisional ball. If you find your first ball in bounds, you can play it and pick up the provisional ball without penalty.

On the Green

There are two reasons to mark your ball (meaning place a ball marker right behind your ball on line with the hole so you can pick up your ball): to clean your ball—which is allowed only on the green—and to prevent your ball from interfering with the putt of any player whose ball is further from the hole.

After everyone has missed those long first putts, the away rule changes, sort of. When your ball is just a couple of feet from the hole, you can hole out or put down a ball marker, pick up your ball, and wait until your ball is again farthest from the hole. Either way, always avoid stepping in the line a player's putt is apt to take when rolling toward the hole.

Finally, when everyone has holed out, the pin is replaced, and everyone leaves the green before the scorekeeper for your group writes down the scores.

You can also clean your golf ball when "clean and replace" is designated at a rain-soaked local course. You may pick up your ball from the fairway (never the rough), clean, and replace it. If your ball sticks in its own pitch mark, pick it up, clean it, and drop it as closely as possible to the spot where it stuck, but never nearer the hole.

Other Helpful Rules

- **Loose impediments.** Twigs, leaves, and anything that can hinder the flight of your ball is an impediment, and loose impediments can be moved. If your ball moves when removing an impediment within one club length of the ball, you receive a one-stroke penalty.
- **Obstructions.** Artificial objects, pavement, sprinkler heads, someone's club accidentally left behind, are obstructions. If it can be easily moved, move it. Or take a drop within one club length of the spot where the ball currently rests, but never nearer the hole.
- **Abnormal ground conditions.** These are "casual" water (water where it isn't supposed to be), ground under repair, or holes dug by burrowing animals. (Dogs don't count as burrowing animals.) Same as obstructions: take a drop, no penalty.
- **Impediment beneath the ball on the green.** In this case, you should mark and lift the ball, remove the debris, and replace the ball. There is no penalty.

Golf Etiquette

If you pick up a copy of the USGA's Rules of Golf, you'll notice that the etiquette section is Section 1. Golf etiquette isn't incidental; it's essential. If you play as we've just described, you'll be fine, but it certainly doesn't hurt to learn a few courtesies that will make your playing partners happy.

Swings, Strokes, and Honors

Don't take a practice swing or make a stroke while anyone within striking distance is around you. Check all directions. With a practice stroke, it's a good idea never to strike at any object on the ground such as a broken tee or pebble; you might just send it hurtling toward a fellow competitor.

Make certain the person with honors is allowed to play first.

Pace of Play

If you and your buddies fall behind by more than one hole to the people playing in front of you, wave the group behind you on through. A two-ball match should be entitled to pass any three- or four-ball match. If you're out on the course alone, a match in front of you may wave you through, but as a single player, you have no standing. So don't get huffy if the foursome in front ignores your very existence.

Swing and Stroke Divots

Any time a swing takes a divot (a slice of turf lifted by a club during a stroke), replace it. Avoid damaging the teeing off area; the same goes in the fairway. Why? Because the rules require the golfer to play the ball where it lies. If your ball rolls into a divot left in the fairway by another golfer, you've got to play it where it lies. You certainly won't be very happy with this situation. Show others the same courtesy you would want.

Golf Carts and Footprints

If you're using a golf cart, obey the notices on the course you're playing. Stay on cart paths where required, and obey the local club rules which will vary sometimes according to ground conditions. Leave the bunker in better condition than you found it. Rake away footprints and craters left by your ball (or someone else's) and the stroke (or strokes).

Damage on the Green

Often a ball landing on the green will leave a ball mark—an indentation—usually with damage to the grass surface. It's far easier to simply watch someone repair a ball mark than to try to explain it. Watch others repair their ball marks. Usually this is done by using a tee or a ball repair implement and lifting the ground back into position, then tamping on it with the putter. Make it a habit to look for and repair other ball marks.

Don't put your golf bag down on the green, because it will leave an indentation. Also, take care when pulling the pin from the hole and replacing it to prevent damage to the edge of the cup. After everyone has holed out, be sure to repair the scuffs on the grass frequently caused by golf shoe spikes.

ALERT!

You may ask your partner, caddie, or your partner's caddie for advice, but not your opponent. According to the USGA, "'advice' is any counsel or suggestion which could influence a player in determining his play . . . choice of club or . . . method of making a stroke."

Playing at the Local Course

All golf courses are different. Obviously the terrain on which each nine- or eighteen-hole course is laid out is different, but the way each course can best be played is different, as well. Each course has its own personality.

It doesn't matter whether you're a member of a posh club that refuses to allow a blade of crabgrass admission on the fairway, or you play on links where the grass seems to have suffered a buffalo stampede, good golf is good golf. Each course has things to offer to your game—things to teach you, and it own sets of challenges.

Fairways

Courses that are flat provide the golfer with the perfect surface for a textbook setup on every shot. Such fairways are easier to hit from than fairways on hilly courses. So, if your home course is flat, you have the ideal surface on which to perfect your ball-striking ability. Diagnosis of flaws is easier because the surface can't be blamed.

Hilly courses, on which flat surfaces for hitting the ball are rare, offer their own sets of advantages. First, such a course can help to teach you about target golf, i.e., the need at times to hit the ball to a spot—usually a flatter spot—rather than to hit the ball as far as you can. Second, you'll learn to compensate for awkward stances in order to make the ball go where you want it to go.

Plush fairways and worn-out fairways each provide lessons. On the former, nine times out of ten the ball will come to rest on a perfect lie for the next shot. A perfect lie will always reward an excellent stroke. On the latter, the ball will often stop beside a clump of grass, or rest on hard, bare ground, forcing the golfer into certain judgments about spin control and the uncertain flight of the ball.

FACT

The design of the course intends to reward good shots and punish the bad. While you should reap the rewards of any course, keep in mind that the further off the fairway your ball strays, the greater the punishment.

Greens

Some courses have greens that are small, flat, and slow, meaning that once a ball lands on the green, the golfer is practically assured of only two putts to hole out. Other courses have undulating greens with slick surfaces, meaning that putting is anything but a cinch. The first type teaches a golfer to fire at the pin with confidence. The second type forces the golfer to target certain sections of the green, perhaps even to ignore the position of the pin, and shoot for a surface some distance away to make certain the ball stays on the putting surface.

Length and Width

Beginning golfers don't always think about these less obvious factors. Long courses encourage a golfer to develop length off the tee and to maximize the distance on every other club for that matter. Shorter golf courses, courses that allow more golfers to get to the green with less trouble, help beginning golfers to learn to score.

Width offers similar lessons, too. The wider the fairways, the easier for the golfer to develop a power game (shots sprayed to the left and right aren't always punished). Narrow courses encourage accuracy, meaning the wisest choice for a golfer is often to sacrifice distance.

Keeping Score

In a round between friends or business associates, scoring is a casual affair. The "marker"—the official title of the "one who is appointed by the 'Committee' to record a competitor's score," according to the USGA's Rule 6—is usually the one who says "I'll keep score."

Keep Up with Your Own Stroke Count

Assume for the moment that you're not the one keeping the official score for your group. You'll be asked after everyone holes out to report your score. Sometimes after an adventurous hole—a hole on which you took the long, scenic route "over the river and through the woods"—you may have to think to be sure. But most of the time, everyone will be able to call out his or her own score for a hole quite readily.

ALERT!

Alas, there seems to be one in every group: the golfer who keeps up with the strokes of each member of the foursome on every hole. Be certain of your score, or prepare to be challenged. Such golfers mean well, but aren't always correct.

The Scorecard

Whether you plan on becoming the marker or not, it is always a good idea to pick up a scorecard in the pro shop before heading to the first tee. Scorecards serve several useful purposes. The first, and most obvious, purpose is that it allows everyone in the foursome to keep up with the scoring. If nothing else, that just adds to the fun of a competitive round. Scorecards also tell you important information about each hole on the course you're about to play, such as distance, shape, and handicap (a good indicator of a hole's difficulty). Scoring is very straightforward as you can see from **FIGURE 1-1**.

FIGURE 1-1

SCORECARD													
REGULAR YARDS	513	145	343	455	140	374	354	352	491	3167			
HANDICAP STROKES	9	15	13	1	11	3	11	5	7				
PAR	5	3	4	4	3	4	4	4	5	36			
NAME: Jim Smith	4	3	5	6	3	5	4	4	5	39			
Joe Doe	5	3	5	6	2	5	6	6	6	44			
	←				B				→				
HOLE NUMBERS	1	2	3	4	5	6	7	8	9	OUT			
REGULAR YARDS	164	553	396	448	409	303	472	185	449	3335	Ⓒ	Ⓓ	Ⓔ
HANDICAP STROKES	18	10	6	2	4	16	12	14	8	IN			
PAR	3	5	4	4	4	4	5	3	4	36	HCP	NET	
Jim Smith	3	6	5	4	6	5	6	3	4	42	12	69	81
Joe Doe	3	6	5	4	6	5	4	4	5	42			
HOLE NUMBERS	10	11	12	13	14	15	16	17	18				

▲ Most scorecards also indicate the shape of each hole along with its length from the tee. This can be helpful when you're playing an unfamiliar course.

Add up each player's score for each hole and total it. Simple, right? Well, sort of—until we throw in handicap.

A Handicap Primer

Handicap golf is the best system ever devised in any sport to allow players of widely differing abilities to actually compete against each other. The USGA Handicap System is generally accepted throughout the United States. The system is based upon the ten best scores from a player's last twenty rounds. To keep it simple, here's the formula used to determine handicap:

The average of the ten best scores over the last twenty rounds, minus the USGA course rating for the course played, times the USGA Slope Rating, divided by 113, equals the USGA Handicap.

Say you take your last ten rounds on your home course and divide that total by ten to get the average score of 90. The scorecard at the club will indicate the USGA Course Rating (which is based on the difficulty of a given course for "scratch" golfers—those who don't require a handicap, such as professionals—and determined by the USGA), which we'll say is

68. The USGA Slope Rating indicates the difficulty of the course for players with a handicap; that is, those who play above-par golf. For our purposes, we'll say the Slope Rating is 100. Hence: [(90 – 68) / 113] × 100 = 9.5 handicap.

QUESTION?

What if I haven't played enough rounds to have a handicap?
If you've never played before and find yourself in a tournament setting, the committee will probably assign thirty-six strokes for a man, and forty strokes for a woman. This method is not a substitute for a USGA handicap, but can be very helpful in an emergency.

Okay, so that's more than you wanted to know about handicap. The value of the handicap is that in stroke play it eliminates strokes from your gross score and yields a very competitive net score. Take a look at the scorecard we showed you earlier.

Chapter 2

What You Need to Get Started

Clubs, balls, shoes, and all the stuff you need to actually get out on the course present a variety of choices, but don't forget that golf is also a mental game. To get started right, knowing what to look for in terms of equipment is important, but approaching the game with the right mental keys is essential.

Developing the Right Mental Game

Most golfers who take lessons begin learning the game with GAP: grip, alignment (stance), and posture, the traditional approach to the first golf lesson. But this isn't always the most important thing to learn first. For instance, the stance used by Lee Trevino has him aiming forty-five degrees to the left of his target, while Sam Snead's stance positioned him forty-five degrees to the right. Many things can be wrong with a beginner's GAP, just as there can be many things wrong with stance and posture of a good pro. But, like great golfers, you'll improve your game despite flaws in your GAP if you first learn to master the mental game of golf.

Watch a pro tournament, and you'll never hear the concepts of a mental game mentioned. Not because these concepts don't matter to the golfing greats, but because they're concepts you just can't see with your eyes on a television screen. Golf is such a mental game—the heart and soul of the game's enjoyment has less to do with the proper materials (clubs, balls, etc.) and more to do with embracing the right concepts.

Before you put a club in your hand, put the following pieces of "equipment" in your mind. They'll wind up being physical tools, tools you will learn about later in the book, but for now lock them in your mind. If you learn to do these correctly, every other golfing skill is secondary.

Club Head Lag

This is the first concept a golfer needs to know. Club head lag is the common denominator in good golf shots. To put it simply, the head of the golf club must lag behind the golfer's hands. Or, try to think of it this way: When the head of the club strikes the golf ball, your hands must be in front of the ball. Imagine a line on the ground extending from the ball to a spot between your feet. Your hands must be ahead of that line when the club face strikes the ball.

When the club head lags behind the hands, the golf club strikes the ball close to the end of the club's downward flight. All shots that are hit off of the ground and into the air must have club head lag. At the professional level, there are a remarkable variety of swings, but the one thing they all do with great consistency is maintain club head lag.

FIGURE 2-1

◄ Your hands should be out in front of the club head at the low point of your swing.

The Low Point of the Swing

Akin to club head lag is the low point of the swing. The low point of the swing is where the club hits the ground. Here's how club head lag and the low point are connected: If your hands are in front of the ball, the swing's low point is closer to the front foot (the left foot for right-handed golfers), or further out in the swing; if your hands are behind the ball, the swing's low point will come before the impact of the club and ball. The low point of the swing should come after impact. The exact spot of the swing's low point will vary according to the club and the shot, but the low point should always come at or after contact with the ball on all shots hit off of the ground.

In many ways this is more of a mental problem than a physical one. Most beginners want to lift the ball into flight. When a golfer thinks about lifting the ball, usually the opposite type of ball flight occurs—the ball skitters across the ground or it goes into the air with much less power and almost no control. Why? Since the golfer is concentrating on getting the ball "up" instead of thinking about the swing's low point, the low point of the swing has moved back toward the right foot.

E ALERT!

Certainly, the proper grip, stance, and posture are extremely helpful in developing a good game, but low point is crucial. When you've been playing golf for a while, examining your swing's low point is a great place to start when sorting out problems with your game.

Many golfers often try to correct their problems with a swing's low point by reasoning that their club is not striking the ball at the proper point because they're standing too far away from the ball, or maybe too close. But a golfer who has mastered the concept of the low point—who has the concept firmly entrenched in his or her mind from the beginning—can stand any distance from the ball and control the low point of the swing.

FIGURE 2-2

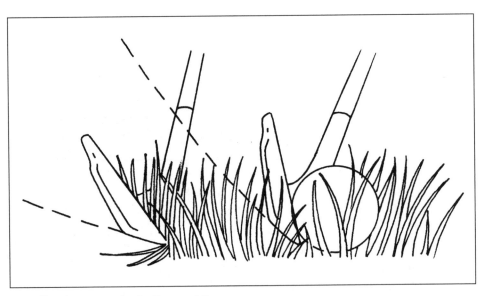

▲ Strike down on the ball to get it up.

Club Face Alignment

Club face alignment affects the direction the ball will travel. Many people make the reasonable (but false) assumption that when addressing the ball, if the club face is square to start, the club face will also be square at impact. But there are many variables acting on that club face which may change its angle before it returns to strike the ball. The angle of the club face will affect the curvature and compression of the ball.

QUESTION?

What does it mean to address the ball?
When a golfer takes a stance and lines up the club to make a stroke, the golfer is said to be addressing the ball.

It's important to understand what the club face should look like throughout a swing, so that a golfer begins to understand how to control the club face angle. We'll discuss this in greater detail later, but for now, keep this concept in the back of your mind.

Clubs and Balls

The golfing equipment industry wouldn't want you to know it, but a pro could play a tournament with "blue-light specials" from the neighborhood discount center and win. Likewise, the worst hacker will still be a hacker even with the finest clubs money can buy. There's very little difference between the worst and the best equipment.

If you're just starting out, you may feel overwhelmed when shopping for equipment, but don't let it get to you. The mental concepts are vastly more important than the "right" or "best" equipment. However, keep in mind that a golfer will play better with clubs and balls he or she believes helps him or her play a better game. You don't have to break the bank (unless of course you want to) to get a set of clubs that will allow you to enjoy golf, improve your game, and score well.

Buying a Set of Clubs

Let's make it easy. Go to your favorite discount store and purchase the tall, rectangular box that includes three iron through wedge; one, three, and five woods; and a golf bag. Prices range from around $150 to a little above $200. Whatever clubs you choose will suit you just fine. Not a single bad shot will be the result of cheap clubs.

Of course, there are some differences in golf equipment. The differences are mostly in the weight distribution in the club heads and in the flexibility of the shaft. And, golf balls have benefited from new technology.

Weight Distribution in the Club Head

Some clubs are designed with the weight in the head of the club evenly distributed. Others are designed with a higher percentage of the weight positioned low, closer to the sole of the club. For most golfers this weight positioning is more noticeable in woods than in irons.

Generally speaking, sole-weighted woods are very good for beginning golfers who have trouble hitting balls into the air. If you have no trouble getting loft on your shots, you'd be better off using clubs with evenly distributed weight in the club heads. If you tend to hit most shots low, consider the clubs with the lower weight distribution.

FACT

You can make your own clubs if you want. There are companies that make excellent components, allowing the avid golfer to select club heads, shafts, and grips to put together just exactly the club type desired.

Some clubs are better in certain situations. For example, if the ground is really hard, irons designed with a wide sole will bounce off hard ground, hampering good ball strike. However, unless the golf course you play is subject to consistently dry or wet conditions, the design of the sole of your irons should be the least of your concerns.

Shaft Flex

The shaft is the "engine" of the club. The faster you swing, the more the club will deform when you hit the ball. So, the slower you swing, the softer (more flexible) a shaft you will want. One type of shaft is not better than the other. Flexibility of golf club shafts varies even among tour players.

It's the ability of the golfer to put together the ingredients of the swing that yields power and distance. A player with excellent mechanics may not need clubs with limber shafts, or the player may make effective changes to his or her swing and discover that a softer shaft better suits his or her game. On the other hand, a more limber shaft in the hands of a golfer already generating plenty of club-head speed is apt to yield less controllable shots.

It's all a matter of feel and need. If your movement is somewhat restricted—your body can't turn as required to generate power, or you're not so physically strong—more flex in a club shaft may be just the ticket to adding distance without a sacrifice of accuracy.

QUESTION?

What's the best shaft for a beginner?
Assess your physical abilities. If you think of yourself as physically strong, consider beginning with stiffer club shafts; if weaker, try more flexible ones. Either way, you will discover that with practice, you'll continue to improve, hitting more consistent shots that are longer and straighter.

Technology and Golf Ball Design

Probably more than any other piece of golfing equipment, it is the golf ball that has changed the most since the mid-1990s. There's so much research being done today with high-speed photography and launch monitors to study dimple configuration and spin rates that the day may soon arrive when a tour player will be "custom fitted" with his or her own model golf ball specifically designed with a dimple pattern suited for his or her unique ball-striking characteristics. Since this technology is not available yet, you needn't worry too much about the design of your golf balls, but there are some things you will want to know.

The Hardness of Golf Ball Covers

Golf balls have either hard or soft covers. Hard-surfaced balls tend to spin less and travel farther. Softer-surfaced balls spin more, but travel less distance. Most pros use—can you guess?—softer-surfaced balls. What does that tell you about the distance most pros achieve?

If you're having trouble hitting the ball straight, if your ball slices wickedly, or if you have a chronic hook, consider using harder balls. Of course, this treats only the symptom and doesn't provide a cure, but it may help enough to provide an extra measure of enjoyment to your game.

How can you know which type you're buying? If the package of balls you're purchasing indicates on the label "durable," "cut resistant," or "distance," you can be sure the ball has a hard cover. In fact, practically all the balls on sale at your local discount department store will be hard-covered balls. The sum of their characteristics makes them the choice of most weekend players.

FACT

Course conditions can make a difference in ball selection. On courses that are softer due to rain or the time of year, golfers who don't hit the ball as far will opt for the harder balls, giving up a measure of control in order to gain a bit of distance. When the ground gets hard, golfers are wise to consider giving up some distance for better spin control.

Putters and Other Gear

Putters are considered "other gear." Since they're clubs, we'll tell you about them first. Shoes and all the rest are less essential parts of the game, although many courses require golf shoes. Of the other golf items, umbrellas and golf gloves are closest to being essentials.

Putters

You may have noticed that some of your buddies have putters that look like weapons from a science fiction movie. If you're just beginning to play the game, those same friends may be too willing to tell you about the "best" putter for you. Don't be fooled; there is no best putter. You should find a putter that feels right for you.

Basically, putters have two different "feels." One type of feel registers a hard "clack" when the putter strikes the ball. The other type of feel, and currently more popular among tour players, is the softer feel of a putter that absorbs a small amount of the collision between putter face and ball. This trend is apt to continue among the best players given the fast condition of most of the greens they play. And more and more, greens everywhere are getting faster. These softer putters have inserts and/or faces that cushion a bit of the initial contact with the ball. Cheap or expensive, find the type that gives you the most confidence.

The Rest of the Gear

Go into any pro shop, golf shop, or large sporting goods store, and you'll find tons of gear. So, what do you really need? And what can you do without? Just look at the list of what we believe are the bare essentials:

- Golf shoes with soft spikes.
- A full-sized golf umbrella.
- Quiet weather gear (clothing that doesn't rustle when you swing).
- Divot tools and ball markers (could be just use a golf tee and a dime).
- Golf bags with a built-in stand.
- Golf glove (okay, this isn't essential—many people do just fine without one).

Finding a Foursome

This isn't as trivial as it seems. The kind of golfers you decide to play with on a regular basis will determine the quality of golf you're destined to play. Most golfers link up with friends from the neighborhood or associates from work, and their golfing marriage is formed, till death or downsizing do they part.

Birds of a Feather Flock Together

As a general rule, the members of a standing foursome tend to evolve into golfers in the same handicap range. High-handicap golfers wind up with other high-handicap golfers, and low with low. It isn't coincidence, rather it's a trait of human nature.

Golfers who cling together tend to have or to develop similar golfing habits. This is somewhat less true of an actual round of golf, and somewhat more true of what members of that foursome do between rounds of golf—what practice habits seem normal for the foursome.

If the individuals comprising your foursome never practice, choosing instead a wide variety of other pursuits, and swing clubs only when they show up for a once a week match, chances are good that habit will become the norm for you, too. If, on the other hand, the individuals in your foursome make it a habit to practice an hour (or ten hours) a week along with the round on the weekends, then that habit will more likely become the norm for you.

Even the approach to playing a round differs according to handicap. Low-handicap golfers plan for shots to make the green in regulation (meaning the specified number of shots to stay at, or above, par) and position the ball on the green for the best chance to hole out. High-handicap golfers plan for shots to stay (or get) out of trouble. The lessons your eyes absorb from your playing partners can definitely affect your game.

Your Golfing Desires

As you take up the game, decide what type of golfer you want to be. The game encompasses all kinds—the handicap system allows every golfer to compete on an even basis. You may even decide that you'll play with one group of friends socially, and another group to hone your competitive skills.

A group of scratch golfers looking for a regular fourth isn't going to make you a permanent fixture in the weekly matches if you have a fifteen handicap (they might if you have a seven handicap, though), so if your plan is to improve your game, be on the lookout for groups with individuals whose handicaps are a few strokes better than yours. In short order, your practice habits and game will approximate theirs.

In general, golfers with twenty-five handicap tend not to practice, except for some occasional extra putting or chipping. Scratch golfers tend to work on various parts of their games, making golf a lifestyle priority.

The Power of Playing Alone

If you're pressed for time, a round of golf played alone may be just the ticket. Or, if you want to get in an extra round a week, you may find that playing alone helps you work on certain parts of your game.

Play with Fewer or More Clubs

Every player has certain clubs he or she has more confidence in than others. Often, instead of hitting a nine iron, for instance, a player will grab an eight iron lower on the shaft and try to achieve the same shorter distance with a full swing, or reduce the swing to attain the same result. There's nothing wrong with this. But when playing alone, with all the pressure off, the time is perfect to take out that club you never touch, or to see if in fact there is another way to use your eight iron.

Of course, you should have practiced with all these clubs and worked on your shots first on the practice range, but there's nothing quite the same as trying out the new shot or club on the course. It's always best to do it alone first, especially if the other folk in your usual group are highly competitive or prone to laughter.

Play an Extra Ball

This is not always a good idea, and on some courses it's frowned upon, but there's probably no golfer alive who hasn't pulled out an extra ball somewhere on the course and given it a whack, either to improve on the first effort or to try to achieve a good result a different way. After all, it's a round alone: It doesn't count—it's play.

Building Confidence on the Practice Range

If you're just beginning to play golf and have just purchased your first set of clubs, you're probably going to take the set out to the range and try them out. Go ahead and surrender to your excitement, but you'll eventually want to settle down and get to business.

The Ultimate Practice

The ultimate practice set consists of only one club. Before all the clubs in your bag will do you any good, you must learn to hit at least one club consistently. (Think of the three mental concepts: club head lag, low point of the swing, and club face alignment.)

FACT

Seve Ballesteros, the great golfing Spaniard, began with only one club, a three iron. He couldn't afford any others. Ben Hogan learned golf early by using only one club for every single shot on the course. When Hogan gained mastery over that club and its many uses, his father suggested he master another club.

The ultimate practice club for beginners—perhaps even for seasoned golfers—is a six iron. Some knowledgeable golfers may argue with that, perhaps suggesting a five iron or a seven iron, but the reasoning behind their arguments is the same: A middle iron—a five, six, or seven iron—allows you to hit the ball far enough to see the curve of the ball in flight. Middle irons also provide for an easier time of converting the three mental concepts (GAP) into physical perfection.

To begin practicing with a three iron, for example, means that more things have to be done right in order to make the ball fly straighter. On the opposite end of the club range, there's so much loft (angle on the face of a club) on a short iron, a nine iron, or a pitching wedge (these irons travel such short distances), it's difficult to get enough feedback when practicing with them to gauge whether or not you're striking the ball properly.

Beginning with a six iron will help you to do the most necessary things well and quicker. The more clubs you start trying to play at the beginning and the longer the clubs you begin with, the less consistent (and probably the less fun) your golf game will be at the start.

Don't Confuse a Warm-Up with Practice

You probably won't want to play those first rounds of golf with your buddies with just a six iron and a putter in your bag; although, it wouldn't be a bad idea. A good strategy for playing the game as a beginner is to behave just like a pro. Head straight to the range before playing a round, and hit some balls with each club.

Hitting balls with lots of different clubs should not be confused with real practice. Real practice involves working with one, maybe two clubs, and striking the ball the same way with the same club over and over until the stroke is grooved (becomes a good repeated swing) and until you're confident.

This isn't the way to practice golf, but it's the best way to warm up before playing. Hit several balls with each club. Reacquaint your mind and your body with how each club feels and what it's like to shift from one club to another.

We'll talk more about drills later, but for now you're equipped with the right tools: the physical and the all-important mental tools. Ⓔ

Chapter 3

The Basic Swing Motion

Have you ever watched a golfer who makes the act of addressing the ball seem as complex as brain surgery? Don't worry, this chapter will show you that the object of the setup is simple, and a good setup is what prepares you for a great swing.

Positioning Your Body for the Setup

You've seen enough golf to have a good idea of how a golfer positions his or her body to set up for a swing. The golfer bends slightly at the waist toward the ball with his or her hands hanging down. This is exactly the place to start on the setup.

Torso Tilt

Leave the clubs in the bag for the moment. Relax your arms and bend a bit from the waist, flexing your knees naturally as you bend. Let your arms just dangle, hanging straight down from your shoulders toward the floor. The ideal tilt is about forty-five degrees from the waist. The tilt needs to feel natural, with no part of the body feeling strain.

Use this visual key: Assuming your belt is parallel to the ground when you're standing erect, your belt makes an excellent indicator of the angle. Don't worry—there are others keys coming.

Hanging Arms

Your arms should be hanging straight down directly from the shoulders on a line to the floor. This is exactly the position you want your arms to be in when gripping the club: straight down, on line from shoulders to fingertips to ground. Remember, you want to attain a stance with no strain on any body part.

To illustrate, try this. Extend your arms out in front of you for a moment, parallel to the ground. It won't be long before your arms will begin to tire at the shoulders and the elbow joints, and your back will begin to ache. Now, bend your torso at that forty-five degree angle with your arms dangling straight down. In this position, you could hold on to a brick and remain comfortable longer than standing with your arms straight out, parallel to the ground. At any arm position other than straight down, you're placing some amount of strain on your arms and shoulders. Throughout a round of golf, the extra bits of fatigue accumulated from every setup with faulty arm position can add up.

The ideal arm position is straight toward the ground. Your hands ought to dangle on a line that places them approximately one to three inches away from your thighs. With all body parts relaxed, the knees flexed, the waist bent, and the arms dangling about an inch away from your thighs, you're very close to the perfect position.

The Shoulder Slant

Hold your position and grab that imaginary club in your hands. Make certain you keep your arms on that straight line from your shoulders to the floor. If a mirror is handy, assume this position in front of the mirror. Get in position first, then take a peek. You'll notice that your right shoulder is lower than your left. This is because your right hand is extended farther down the club than your left.

FACT

If you've done everything right so far and have found a comfortable position, your hips will be tilted just the right amount. As you flexed your knees and bent from the waist, your rear should naturally have stuck out further, as though you were starting to sit down on a bar stool. If it didn't, then imagine you're sitting against the edge of that stool.

Knee and Ankle Flex

Knee flex almost naturally occurs when you tilt your torso and slant your shoulders, and so does the ankle flex . . . almost. You want your ankles to flex to the point that you feel the proper pressure between your feet and the ground.

Roll up onto the balls of your feet and stand on your toes. You'll notice that as the pressure shifts toward your toes, your knees straighten in order to keep the body comfortably balanced. Your body naturally seeks balance, and a natural balance is precisely what you're looking for in your golf stance.

Tilt your torso, hang your arms, slant your shoulders, and flex your knees as we just described, and now flex your ankles as though you were wearing a pair of ski boots. Feel the pressure on the bottom of your feet. Flex your ankles until you feel the floor most strongly between the arches of your feet and the balls of your feet. That's the position at which your lower body is lined up best.

Foot Position

Comfort, stability, and strength remain the watchwords all the way down through your feet. Should your feet be rigidly parallel to each other in your stance? That isn't the most comfortable or most stable position, is it? Turn the toes on both feet out slightly. Don't overdo it, but make it comfortable.

With the toes turned out, your hips will rotate better over your center of gravity, which is good. With both feet parallel or pigeon-toed, your hips slide from side to side more easily, disrupting your center of gravity, which is not good.

Head and Neck Tilt

The function of the setup is to help the golfer swing consistently and focus all possible power to the ball and club face at impact. Another equally important part of the swing deals with keeping the ball in the vision of both eyes at all times during the swing. Your head must be positioned so that it's tilted forward and both your eyes are looking directly at the ball. To see the ball properly, don't move your eyes to find the ball, move your head until your eyes are sighting directly at the ball.

This head and neck tilt will have a big affect on shoulder turn. If your head is too high and your eyes must look down to find the ball, your shoulder turn will be too flat. If your head is too low and your eyes must look up to see the ball, your shoulder turn will be too steep.

Tilt your head slightly toward your back foot. Turning your head too much toward your back foot will increase your shoulder turn and thus increase your chances of hitting a high shot with reduced distance. Leaning your head toward the target decreases your shoulders' ability to turn, making it harder for you to get shots into the air.

How do you know when you have just the right amount of head tilt?
Shut your left eye. If you can keep your right eye on the ball at all points of your swing, your head is tilted to the right just enough. In fact, you'll want to include this as a practice drill—hitting balls with your left eye shut. The ball should never shift to peripheral vision.

Club Height and Shaft Angle

Once your body is in the correct position, your next step is to get the club in the correct position. There's a single correct height for every club. In other words, even though your clubs aren't all the same length, the distance from the ground to the butt of your club (once in position) will always be the same. There is also a single correct position for your hands, and it stays the same for every club as well.

The Club and Your Zipper

Pull two clubs from your bag: the six iron and the driver. Start with the six iron, and position yourself in the proper alignment allowing the club to rest naturally on the ground. Assuming your stance is correct, the butt end of the club should point toward the base of your trousers' zipper.

Now, get in the right position with the driver. You'll notice that when you have properly aligned the club height (pointed at the base of your trousers' zipper), the only pair of variables are the position of the club head on the ground and the angle of the shaft. The head of the driver is farther away from your body than the head of the six iron was. The angle of the shaft of the longer club is less than the angle of the six iron (measuring from the ground). Try the same drill with a wedge for another point of reference.

Your Hands and Your Trouser Crease

You now have the height of the club and the height of your hands in an easily repeatable alignment. The distance of your hands away from your body should be a natural movement associated with ankle and knee flex, hip tilt, and your bend at the waist. There is, however, one last position of your hands to be concerned about at setup: the proximity of your hands in relation to both of your legs. Should your hands be more closely aligned with your left leg or your right leg?

> Your stance should feel comfortable, balanced, and strong. You will be bent about forty-five degrees from the waist, and approximately the same amount at the hips, with arms on line from your shoulders to the ground, one to three inches in front of your thighs.

Your hands should be aligned so that when gripping the club, the back side of your left hand is just inside the crease on the left leg of your trousers. From the position where your hands have naturally hung, they'll have to be moved slightly to the left to align with the crease in the left leg of your pants. This posture and hand position does not change regardless which club (except the putter, of course) you are preparing to use.

Distance from the Ball

A lot of beginning and intermediate golfers first determine how far to stand from the golf ball and then make everything else about their swing conform to the distance. This is incorrect. When you set up properly, the length of each club will dictate precisely the body's distance from the ball. Put your hands in the right position, tilt the body properly, and make the small adjustments necessary with your feet to approach the ball.

The club and body positions will have you zeroed in perfectly for every shot. If your hands are only a couple of inches from your leg, your arms are hanging straight down, and your body is tilted at a forty-five degree angle, the head of the club will fall where the ball is supposed to be.

Play the driver off the front heel; all the rest are two inches behind. Be sure to keep your hands aligned with the trousers' crease for every normal shot. Do not shift your hands for each club. This will vary the low point of the swing and make for inconsistent shots.

FIGURE 3-1

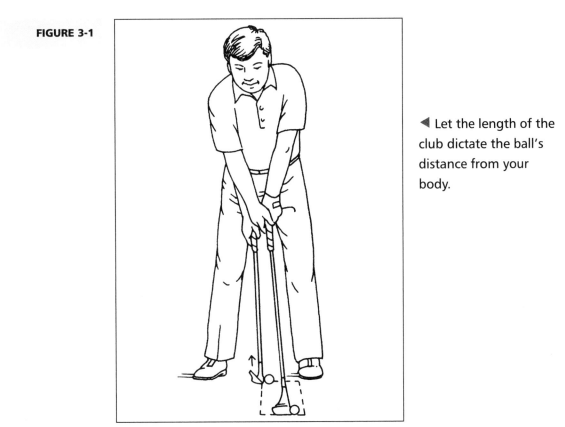

◀ Let the length of the club dictate the ball's distance from your body.

Gripping the Club

The terms "strong" and "weak" are used when referring to the grip and are meant to describe the position of the hands. When one or both hands are rotated clockwise, the grip is considered strong. When rotated counter-clockwise, the grip is weak. The ideal grip is neither too strong nor too weak.

Place the palm of your left hand flat against the front of your left thigh. Now, keeping your pinkie on your thigh, rotate the thumb side of your hand one quarter-turn counterclockwise. This motion puts your hand at a forty-five degree angle, with your pinkie on your thigh and thumb in the air. This is the angle at which you want your left hand to grip the club.

Now grip the club with your left hand, taking care to maintain that forty-five degree angle. The shaft should nestle more snugly in your curled fingers than in your palm. This means you'll be better able to hinge your wrists. Now that you know how to properly align your left hand on the club, it's time to add your right hand.

Grip the club in the fingers of your right hand and notice the **V** formed at the base of the right thumb and forefinger. The **V** should point at a spot between your right ear and right shoulder (as will the **V** formed with your left hand).

FIGURE 3-2

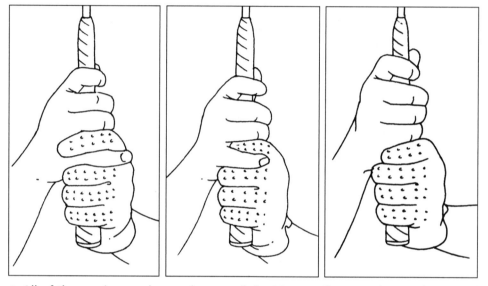

▲ All of these grips can be used successfully. Most golfers use the overlap grip or nine-finger grip (center). Fewer golfers use the ten-finger grip (right). Fewer yet use the interlocking grip (left).

How Tight to Hold the Club

The tighter you hold a golf club, the less flexible your wrists become and the slower the club head will be able to impact the ball. More tension on the grip means the ball will not carry as far. You'll want to hold the club as tight as necessary to control the club, but not much more than that. Longer hitters hold the club more loosely.

The Pressure Point

The constant contact between your left thumb and its point of contact with the right palm is important to your grip. This pressure point should stay constant all the way through your swing. To lose that connection between your left thumb and right palm means that your elbows are farther apart at impact than at address.

As a practice drill, place the pointed end of a golf tee where your thumb and palm touch as you grip the club. Then swing the club or hit some balls. If the tee comes out, you haven't kept the contact, and your elbows are pulling apart in your swing.

Reduce the Target Distance

In football, the quarterback may throw to a target fifteen to fifty yards away. In basketball, a player may shoot at a basket two to twenty-five feet away. In soccer, a player may kick at a target several yards wide from twenty yards or so. In golf, you aim at a target 450 to 1,500 feet away. And you've got to aim with a long stick in your hands, while standing sideways to the target! Quite a bit of difference, wouldn't you say? This is why good aim is so important.

The first thing a golfer must do is reduce the target distance. This is one of those unexpected times when high school geometry comes in handy. A straight line can be made using any two points. In this example, our points are the golf ball and the flag.

Some golf instructors call it psychological vision: training your vision to see only the straight line that is necessary for the perfect golf shot. If your eyes spend time sizing up the bunker on the left, the creek along the right, and that huge tree that should be out of play, you can guess which direction the ball is least likely to go.

To do this most effectively, stand several strides behind your golf ball and on line with the target. You become the first point on the line, with your golf ball now along the line between you and the flag. With your sight along this line, pick a point on the line three to six feet out in front of the ball, such as a broken golf tee or a blade of grass.

Walk back to the ball, place the head of the club on the ground behind the ball, and line the club head up, square to the new, nearer target. Set your feet and assume your stance. Now you're ready to hit the ball.

FIGURE 3-3

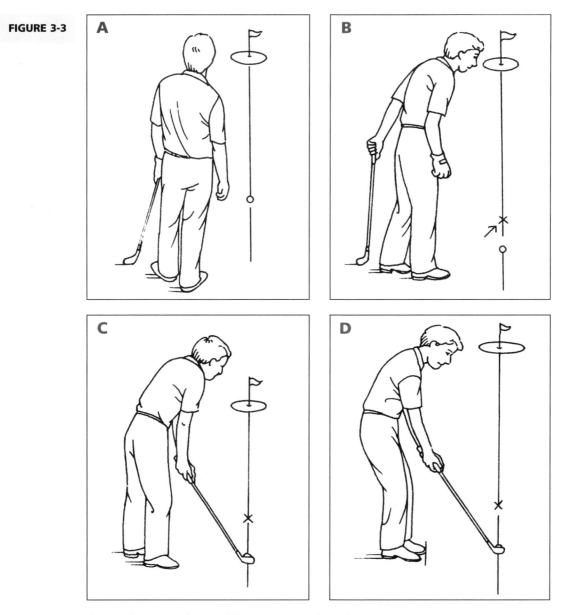

▲ Develop a routine and line up every shot the same way.

Keep Both Eyes on the Ball

An old adage that anyone who has ever played sports has heard is "Keep your eye on the ball." The truth is, it's best to keep *both* eyes on the ball in golf.

Use Your Binocular Vision

Without a club in your hand, stand as though you were addressing a golf ball. Place a ball on the ground roughly where it would be if you were about to hit it. Now, rapidly wink one eye and then the other, back and forth, back and forth. The stationary ball appears to move. The eyes, each focusing on the ball from a different perspective, give us vision in three dimensions.

To find out which eye is your dominant eye, create a triangle with your thumbs and forefingers. Line up a distant object in the center of the triangle. Close one eye and note the location of the object in the triangle. Then do the same thing with the other eye. Whichever eye keeps the object closest to the center of the triangle is your dominant eye.

Both eyes ought to remain on the ball throughout the entire golf shot. Put a club in your hands, draw the club head back from the ball, and stop at the top of your backswing. Assuming you are right-eye dominate, close your left eye. (If you are left-eye dominate, you should close the right eye.) Is the ball still in view? If not, your shots will lack consistency. That ball—beginning in view of both eyes, switching to one-eyed vision, and then back to both eyes—has, in effect, become a moving target. Exercises in a later chapter will help keep you flexible enough for a long backswing and good binocular vision. Right now, do your best to simply keep both eyes on the ball.

Don't Let Your Binocular Vision Trick You

Try to find a long stretch of straight railroad track to stand on. If you don't want to bother, just envision it. If you were to stand between the tracks and look down the parallel lines, the tracks would never converge in your sight. Now turn sideways so that your feet point toward one of the rails. Turn your head down the track. The parallel tracks seem to come together.

We've already solved this problem for long golf shots (by locating a target close to the ball), but it can also be a problem on putts. A fraction of an inch can make the difference between holing out and lipping out (the ball hits the rim but doesn't fall in).

Many golfers, after standing behind their putts to get the line, will line up the print on the ball exactly on the line they will use to strike their putt. They've used their binocular vision twice. First, to gain perspective from behind the ball, and a second time to line up the name of the ball on their intended line using both eyes. Now when standing over the ball, all they have to do is make the club stroke on the line.

FIGURE 3-4

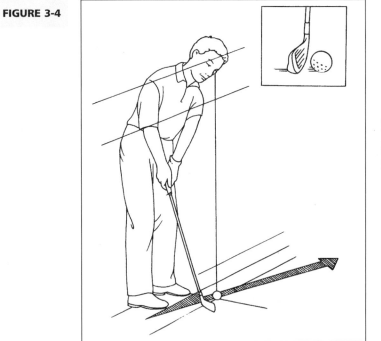

◀ Establish an intended line for each putt using your binocular vision.

Putting the Body in Motion

To a beginner, all these ingredients seem to complicate what should be a natural motion. However, there are many motions the body could be trained to accept as natural. Any golfer can put together a string of twists and jerks of the wrong sort and still hit a ball straight some of the time; but, do the swing right, and you'll learn to hit straight shots that also have power.

Shoulder Motion

The role of the shoulders is possibly the most neglected part of the swing motion. There are those who contend that the hands will keep the shoulders in place, suggesting that the shoulders are just going along for the ride. But in viewing countless golfing swings, one of the things that holds true is that the people who keep the swing in the right path are the people whose shoulders repeat their own path on every swing.

ALERT!

Although you're learning the proper swing one body part at a time, you can't practice the proper shoulder motion as a stand-alone part of the swing. Your ability to make your shoulders repeat their proper paths each time is directly connected to the movement of your hips.

The Path of the Front Shoulder

Think of the shoulder closest to the target as the "front" shoulder. In the address position, the front shoulder should be parallel to the target line and roughly parallel with the feet and the knees. In the swing, the front shoulder will turn ninety degrees until it is pointing down toward the ground.

A basic rule of thumb is to get your front shoulder to turn just behind the golf ball. First be sure you're thinking rotation, with your head as the center of the circle and your shoulder as a point on the circle. You'll be bringing your shoulder down, and it will turn just behind the ball. Take care not to sway to the right, drawing your shoulder along a horizontal path to align it with the ball.

The Path of the Back Shoulder

One key to getting the front shoulder rotating properly is to rotate the back shoulder properly. Many golfers pull the club away from the ball, allowing the back shoulder to slide along a horizontal path. This is incorrect. Instead, make the back shoulder rotate up along that circular path.

FIGURE 3-5

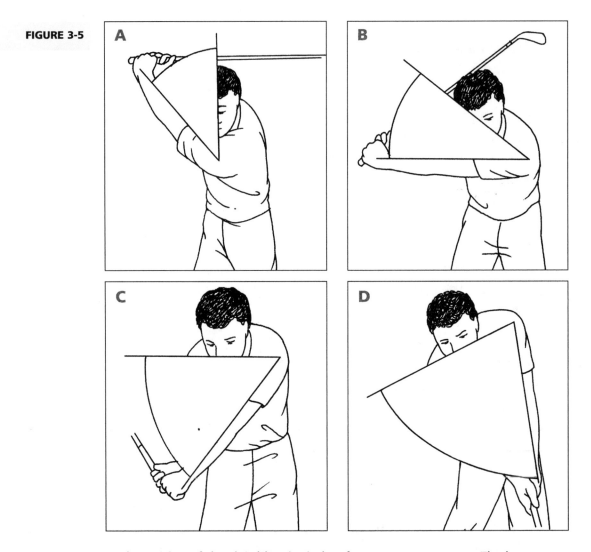

▲ The motion of the shoulders is vital to faster arm movement. The less shoulder rotation, the less power in the shot.

Once the shoulders have taken the correct path by rotating to the top of the backswing, think "pull." Your front shoulder should pull the swing toward impact rather than your back shoulder pushing the club toward impact, and your shoulders will rotate in an almost identical path back to and through the start.

Muscle Coil for Turning Speed

The secret to generating turning speed through muscle coil is to rotate the swing around a fixed axis. In the case of the golf swing, that fixed axis is the spine. To illustrate, grip a golf club, stand perfectly upright, and bury the butt of the club in your navel so that the club is parallel to the ground. Now, twisting only from the spine with the hands and the club stationary at the belly, make the club swing back and forth.

Continue to make the club move and slowly bend over. The fixed axis hasn't changed. The club is still rotating around your spine, but you'll notice that there are certain motions in your ankles, knees, legs, and hips that now come into play, aiding your swing around that fixed axis. The less side-to-side or up-and-down body motion a golfer has, the less power is dissipated and the more efficiently it is concentrated around that axis. The more the rotation of the shoulders around a pivot point and the less side-to-side sway, the better all the rest of the body parts will transmit energy from the muscles to increase club-head speed.

Examples of a Fixed Axis

Here's an image that has nothing to do with golf, but everything to do with generating the same kind of power your golf swing needs. Even if you haven't been to a carnival, you've surely seen the shooting gallery depicted in movies: the ducks on a conveyer "swimming" from one side to the other. They move along at a slow but constant speed, then at the end of the conveyer belt, just as they start to turn under, they whip around with much greater speed than they were traveling while dodging ammo. The conveyer speed doesn't change, but these hinged ducks speed along for an instant when they get to that fixed axis.

Coiling the Muscles Around the Axis

Using an imaginary club, address the ball. Settle in to the stance as it has been formed up to now: torso tilt, and knee and ankle flex. Rotate the shoulders to the top of the backswing, concentrating on wrapping your muscles around the axis. Hold at the top of the backswing. What do you feel?

If done properly, you should feel muscular tension up the inside of your front leg and throughout your entire back leg all the way into your rear end. The muscles of your front side, up your back, and through the outside of your front shoulder and upper arm should feel taut. You should notice a mild protest in the muscles of your back as well as your shoulders, arms, and back side. If this is what you feel, you're coiled to unleash a lot of power, especially if you can release that power around the axis.

FIGURE 3-6

▲ When you turn your body around the fixed axis of the spine, you're loading up torque, as if you were winding up a spring.

Balance and Weight Shift

Over the past three decades, much scientific research has been applied to golfing mechanics. Even so, there's some disagreement about the amount of weight shift that ought to take place from address to backswing to follow-through.

Some excellent teachers of the game will now say that the weight should stay balanced between the feet, and that the legs have much less to do with the power of the golf swing than once was thought. Other excellent teachers continue to hold that the weight of the golfer should shift during the swing from centered between the feet, to mostly on the right leg at the top of the backswing, to mostly supported by the left leg at follow-through. Regardless of the disagreement about weight shift, teaching pros are unanimous about the muscles coiling around an axis as nearly fixed and stationary as possible.

FACT

There's nothing odd about the perfect set-up body position for a golf shot. When the tilts and flexes are right, your body is in a very strong and balanced position—a position you'll be able to repeat over and over without a thought. This is the position in which your center of gravity is most stable.

Hand Path

FIGURE 3-7

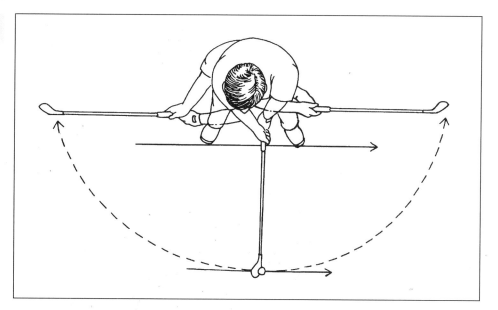

▲ Your hands should be an extension of the club. The position of the club face should be in line with the back of the top hand on the club at all parts of your swing.

The hands have one primary role in the golf swing: to hold on to the club. The hands become part of the club; they *do not* swing the club. To get a picture of the path the hands take on the downswing, imagine a string attached to the inside quarter of the ball and running straight up to the butt of the club at the top of the backswing. Your hands should move directly down that straight piece of string.

Elbow Motion

The motion of the elbow is probably the greatest key to uncoiling the backswing and striking the ball consistently. The most successful golfers have the back elbow in one of two positions on the downswing: either down at the side or slightly in front of the back hip. Keep the back elbow from sticking out away from the body at the top of the swing. The most significant key to keeping the elbow in the right position is to make certain that, from address through impact, the right and left elbows remain the same distance apart.

Start your downswing with a "hitch" in your left hip. Let your left hip shift slightly forward. This will put your elbow in the proper position to make solid contact with the ball.

One trick to keeping the elbows the right distance apart is to put a volleyball between your elbows when you address the ball. If the volleyball stays in place through the backswing, downswing, and impact, you're much more apt to hit the ball toward your target. If the back elbow separates from the front at the top of the backswing, you're apt to pull the ball and send it on a straight line well to the left of the target, or slice the ball and send it curving wickedly to the right.

Knee Motion

Your knees begin on their own line parallel to the target line. By the time you reach the top of your backswing, the front knee has moved behind the ball, while the back knee points at the ball, helping to keep the body turning around its fixed axis. On the downswing, the front knee moves forward as the hips rotate, and the back knee should end up pointing at the front knee.

Motion of the Right Wrist

To get a clear picture of right-wrist issues, grab a club and aim at an imaginary target. Stand behind the ball, pick out your distant target and an intermediate one a few feet in front of the ball, and line up the club face with the intermediate target. Obviously, you want the club face to return to this exact position when it strikes the ball. If all the other parts of the swing are intact, releasing the right wrist at just the right time ensures a square club face at impact—and an accurate shot.

At impact, with the club face square, your right wrist will be positioned just as it was at address. Now, draw the club through the first two or three feet of the backswing and slowly return the club to the ball, but begin to release your cocked wrist too early. You'll hear some call it "pronation," or "rolling the wrist." This just means that your right wrist is rolling/pronating/releasing from right to left too early.

When the wrist pronates early, the club face will be closed (angled toward the body) at impact, which usually results in a hook. This is often a problem when striving hard to get more power into the swing.

Draw the club back again. This time don't let the wrists return to their original position at address. You'll notice that the angle on the club face is open (faced away from the body). Late release of the right wrist causes the ball to slice.

Chapter 4

Teeing Off

You may already know that there's something a little different about teeing off. Perhaps you believe that teeing off is easier than any other golf shot. But that doesn't mean you're hitting off the tee properly or as well as you can. This chapter will show you how to make the most of your teeing experiences.

The Raised Ball

Not all balls hit from the tee are raised. (A raised ball is a ball that's not in contact with the ground.) On shorter par threes, for example, a tee is used to ensure the perfect lie, and the excellent player will push the tee all the way into the ground. A ball's contact with the ground has a lot to do with how the ball will carry in the air.

The best way to hit the raised ball is with the same type of swing you use for a ball on the ground, but with an important difference. Instead of hitting the ball at or just before the swing's low point, you've got to hit the ball just after the low point. You've got to hit up on it.

FACT

Perhaps you've seen a golfer "back" his or her shot up on the green. The ball carries fifteen feet past the hole because the golfer has determined that's the perfect place for the ball to land. Then the golfer counts on the ball's spin to bring the shot back toward the hole.

Hitting Up

The only time you ever hit up to strike a golf ball is when the ball is raised on a tee. For every other golf shot, you should hit down on the ball. In other words, when hitting a raised ball, the low point of your swing comes behind the ball; whereas when hitting off the ground, the low point of the swing comes at or slightly in front of the ball.

Position the Ball

You won't change your swing to make this work, nor do you need to change your stance. The primary change is in the position of the ball. You're going to position the ball to be struck at a different part of the swing.

There are some shots played with the ball farther back in your stance and more toward your right foot, but most of your golf shots will be played from roughly two inches inside your left foot. That's because the low point of the swing occurs around there.

To hit up on the ball means to move the ball forward in your stance so that your natural swing is past its natural low point when the ball is struck. Basically, you use a longer club so the ball will be farther away from your body, and you hit it at a different point of your swing, but the swing is the same swing.

Assume your stance for a moment. The hitting-up position of a ball on a tee will move the ball forward so that the ball is in line with your big toe's joint in the ball of your left foot.

FIGURE 4-1

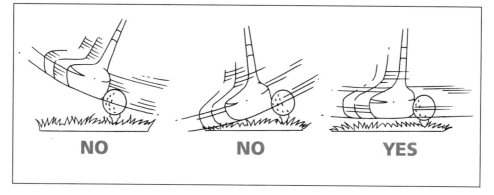

NO   NO   YES

▲ The driver strikes the ball just after the swing's low point. Get the low point consistent (about two inches inside of your front heel), and teeing off becomes a cinch. If the ball is forward of the low point, you'll catch it just right for carry and roll.

How the Ball Behaves

When a tee shot is properly struck, the ball leaves the tee with topspin rather than backspin. Unlike balls on the fairway that get their lift from the down stroke and the ground, a tee shot gets its lift from the slight upward angle of the club at the beginning of the upswing.

The topspin generated does not overcome the slight angle of the club "lifting" the ball into the air. If you hit the ball too far into the upswing, the ball may still leap into the air, but it will almost immediately dive into the ground. If you hit the ball too close to the end of the downswing, the ball may skitter directly across the ground.

Golfers who repeatedly tee the golf ball too far toward the back foot find that they top the ball sometimes, and other times they'll send the ball high into the air and cause the shot to be very short. When the ball is hit at just the right time in the upswing, it launches out and up into the air, and when it hits the ground, it will roll for even greater distances because of its topspin.

Not all the best players hit tee shots with topspin. Watch a tournament and pay attention to the roll the pros get off tee shots. Some play their tee shots to get lots of roll; others get very little. A few of the very longest drivers of the ball get almost no roll.

Positioning the Body to Hit Up

The position of the body and the motion of the swing stays the same whether hitting off the ground or off a tee . . . almost. You may discover that one or all three of these minor shifts will improve your ability to hit off a tee. But first, a word of caution: Don't over analyze the differences between the basic swing motion and hitting up on the ball. The trick is to keep very nearly the same swing and merely reposition the ball so that the club makes contact at a different part of the swing.

This isn't as easy as it sounds. There are plenty of experienced players who make far too many adjustments between hitting off the ground and hitting a tee shot. Some will begin with too much weight on the forward foot because the ball is placed forward. Some shift their hands to align with the shot. Some stand more erect or straighten their arms out away from the body, so that their arms no longer hang at a more natural angle straight down from the shoulders.

Now that your attention has been called to these adjustments, you're likely to notice them on the course, and you'll notice some players who seem to get away with it. You may wonder why and how. It's most likely that because they play so much golf, they're able to make all sorts of improper adjustments and still hit the ball with a level of consistency simply by sheer repetition of their efforts.

Repositioning the Spine

Try this. Grab an imaginary six iron and line up a golf shot using an imaginary ball resting near the middle of your stance. Now let your imaginary six iron grow into a driver and reposition it behind the teed ball located near the big toe of your front foot. (Remember to keep your hand position along your left leg and an inch or so from your body.) Transform that club back into a six iron and line up the first imaginary shot. Repeat this cycle a few times, and you may notice that when you move from the six iron to the driver, your spine actually shifts slightly toward your back foot. The key word is "slightly." You'll probably feel it more than you can see it.

Now think about the swing for a second. The swing creates an arc that has a low point designed to strike the ball and then the ground on your six iron shot. By tilting the spine and keeping the same swing, we've changed that arc just enough to ensure that you'll hit up on the ball. Chances are, your body will come close to making that adjustment naturally.

FACT

When struck properly, a ball on the fairway is "pinched" between the downward force of the club head and the ground, causing the ball to fly up into the air and move toward its target with backspin. Strike a ball in the sand the same way and you're apt to remain in the sand.

A Shift in the Stance

Keeping the imaginary ball, grab a real six iron and set up for your imaginary shot. Once you've lined it up, take a swing. Set up for another six iron shot, but grab your driver. Without changing anything but the ball position (and maybe the tilt of your spine), hit that tee shot. It may not have felt quite so comfortable to you.

Before you analyze why, step away from your imaginary ball, then address it again with the driver and take your swing. If that felt more balanced and more comfortable, your body may have made its own slight adjustment.

If you were to measure the distance between your feet, you may have found that your feet are slightly wider apart when you prepare to hit with the driver. This difference in stance won't be enormous. In fact, it may not be noticeable to someone watching, but it will be noticeable to the golfer—in terms of both balance and the power he or she is able to generate.

Foot Position

Grab that imaginary driver and assume your stance with both feet turned slightly outward (ducklike) and toes touching an imaginary line that is parallel to the target. When you're comfortable and ready to hit the perfect tee shot, pivot your back foot so that it's now perpendicular to the target line, while keeping your club at address position. You'll notice a slight weight shift and a different feel all the way up your back leg. Many golfers use this stance for almost all shots. Others find it helpful on the drive because it helps to turn the body better through the ball.

Get into the groove of the basic swing first—hitting the ball off the ground. Then learn to hit the teed ball, making certain you make any adjustments subtly and only one at a time.

Weight Transference

You'll get some argument about weight transference from golf instructors when it comes to the basic swing motion and hitting most golf shots. Some will say the weight stays balanced around that fixed axis (the spine). Others will insist that during the progression of the swing, there is (or should be) a shift from weight centered between the feet to weight centered over the instep of the back foot, then returning on the downswing to the middle of the stance, and finally forward, centered over the instep of the front foot.

You'll also get some argument about weight shift while driving the ball, but less. Even though the concept of the fixed axis is sound, using a driver with the longer shaft and heavier head, and hitting up on the ball, all mean that the body must do a few things a little differently.

Begin with Balance

On occasion you'll see a pro lose his or her balance on a golf shot and recover by coming out of the follow-through using the front foot as a stabilizer. Even with a shift in your body weight during the sequence of the swing, your stance should remain stable enough to endure a gentle shove without causing you to lose your balance.

Weight Shift Around the Fixed Axis

Address that imaginary tee shot again, only this time assume your stance so that your buttocks are just touching a wall. Begin your backswing. Immediately you'll notice that your left buttock lifts from the wall and your right buttock presses more firmly against the wall.

Your hips are rotating so that at the top of your backswing, with your front shoulder pointing directly at the ball and your back shoulder pointing straight up to the sky, your hips will be at forty-five degrees. Your body is rotating around your spine. Your weight has shifted so that now the weight is centered on a line from your back foot up through the inside of your back leg.

ALERT!

If your body sways to create your weight shift, you can't generate as much power as you can by shifting your weight around that fixed axis. Remember the shooting gallery ducks "whipping" around the pivot point at the end of the conveyer? You want your club whipping around your pivot point, too.

Now, begin your downswing and notice your buttocks roll across the wall, rotating around your spine as the weight shifts. Finish your follow-through and notice that your rotation has shifted so that your right buttock is completely clear of the ball and your weight is centered up your right leg. If a gentle shove in your follow-through position would cause you to fall forward, you've shifted your weight too much.

FIGURE 4-2

▲ Your swing begins with your weight centered. By the top of the backswing your weight has shifted toward the inside of your back leg. On the downswing, your weight begins to shift forward so that at the finish, your weight is centered over the inside of your front leg.

Getting the Weight to Shift Forward

Get back against the wall again with your imaginary club at the top of the backswing, one buttock pressed into the surface, and the other rotated away from the wall. If you start the downswing with your arms, what happens? Initially your right buttock stays pressed into the wall and attempts to slide sideways, and the weights stays on your back foot.

If your instincts tell you something is wrong, your instincts are right. You're setting up a golf swing that will do one or more of three bad things: top the ball, bounce the club head off the ground behind the ball, or greatly reduce your power by keeping the weight back.

So, what should begin the downswing and weight shift? The hips. Some golfers call it a "hitch," which refers to moving the hips forward first. From your position against the wall, this means sliding the hips forward toward the target first. It's not a long slide but a very short one.

Get at the top of your backswing and let the rotation of your left hip back toward the wall be the charge that detonates your downswing. Try it. Releasing your hips from their forty-five degree angle at the top of the backswing and sending your front hip back toward the wall—releasing your hips at the first part of your downswing—causes your shoulders to begin to turn and the weight to begin its roll across the spinal axis toward the follow-through.

Avoiding Danger from the Tee

There you stand at the tee. You're behind the ball, picking out your target, and then picking out the closer target (the one that's three to six feet in front of the ball). You're ready to smack the drive. Then, just before you address the ball, you notice a lake on the right. You're doomed.

The Inferior Solution

A great golf course is designed to toy with your mind. A good golf course blatantly declares what it will give you and what its dangers are; it challenges the golfer to try to keep his or her mind on the opportunities without obsessing on the dangers. For instance, if there's a huge lake lining the right side of the fairway or a single tree overhanging the fairway on the left at just about the height your driver usually flies from the tee, those obstacles will likely be in your mind when you line up for your tee shot.

Tee up on the side of the tee box closest to the danger. If there's a creek along the right, tee up on the right of the tee box. If there's an overhanging tree along the left, tee up on the left. This has the effect of sending your tee shot off at an angle away from the trouble rather than parallel to or even slightly in the direction of trouble.

Suppose the intended target of your tee shot is a spot in the middle of the fairway, and your consistent swing allows you to send most of your golf shots straight. If you were to hit toward the middle of the fairway from the middle of the tee box, your ball will travel parallel to that creek on the right. If your ball carries to the right of the target line, then it may be heading for trouble. On the other hand, if you were to tee the ball on the side of the tee box nearest the creek, and hit the ball toward the same fairway target, your ball will take flight on an angle, sending it away from trouble. That extra angle for error could come in handy.

So, why is this an inferior solution? While the concept is excellent, the problem is that it may cause you to focus too much on trouble and not enough on making a good shot.

FACT

When you see a pro tee the ball near one of the tee markers—sometimes even with the tee marker between his or her feet and the ball—the pro isn't doing it to avoid trouble, but rather because the perfect shot he or she has envisioned requires that particular angle from the tee.

The Superior Solution

The best way to avoid trouble from the tee is not to "see" it. In the mid-1990s, a major college golf team was leading its conference tournament with several other teams in hot pursuit. The coach of this university's golf team called his players together, and, among other things, said to them: "Just play good golf, and whatever you do stay away from that tree on number seventeen." You can guess the single obstacle on the course that created the problems and cost the team the championship.

If you're busy cluttering your mind with all the potential disasters your tee shot could find, chances are excellent you'll find one of them. As one collegiate golf coach has observed, if you see the tree on the left, the fairway in the middle, and the lake on the right, your brain is giving you only a $33\frac{1}{3}$ percent chance of landing in the fairway.

Develop a positive pre-shot routine. When you stand behind your tee shot to pick your target, screen out everything that will prevent you from hitting exactly the kind of shot you plan to hit. Then, with the confidence that comes from having grooved your stroke, take the perfect practice swing. Address the ball and hit the shot you've rehearsed. Otherwise, if you're are afraid to draw the club back, you're already in trouble and you're headed toward danger.

FACT

Satchel Paige, baseball Hall of Famer, made a statement about his age that ties in perfectly to avoiding danger on the golf course. Instead of age, avoiding danger on the golf course " . . . is a matter of mind over matter. If you don't mind, it don't matter."

When to Leave the Driver Alone

If you've played a handful of rounds with some inexperienced golfers, you may have noticed that some of them never pull their drivers from the golf bag, choosing instead to hit a three wood or an iron off every tee. Most golfers who leave the driver in the bag do so because they're afraid to hit it. If you have it in mind to continue to improve as a golfer, use all your clubs. You'll become a better golfer learning to use all of your clubs instead of becoming dependent on only three or four clubs. If the hole you're about to play calls for length off the tee, whip out the driver and let the big dog eat.

There are some circumstances, however, that call for other decisions, such as a hole where the tee shot needs to carry over a distant bunker or a creek. Experience has taught you that with the wind at your back or when the air is hot, your tee shot carries the hazard easily. But today, the wind is in your face and the air is cold. Using a shorter club to stay on the near side of the hazard and planning to use a longer club for the second shot is the wiser play. Or, if the fairway is quite narrow out at the distance where your tee shot usually lands, the same concept applies. Hitting a tee shot short of the narrow area becomes a feasible alternative.

A great tee shot isn't necessarily the longest tee shot of the foursome. A great tee shot is the tee shot that comes to a stop in a place that provides the golfer the best opportunity to get the ball close to the pin while taking most of the trouble out of play.

Chapter 5

Improving Your Accuracy

There are only two ingredients affecting the flight of the ball to the left, middle, or to the right: the swing path and the face angle of the club. This chapter will show you how to correct a faulty swing path or face angle for improved accuracy on every shot.

Swinging Inside-Out

You already know the basic swing motion. Now let's take a look at the proper swing path. The swing that is on path is the inside-out swing. At address, the club face is perpendicular to the target line. Since the axis around which you will swing is not directly suspended on top of the ball, the instant the club moves away, it moves off of and inside the target line. In order for the club to return to that lined-up position at address, it must approach the ball on the downswing on an inside-out path. In fact, the proper swing path will cause the club to strike the inside quarter of the ball.

Swing Path

To get the club consistently on path, the back elbow must define that path for the shaft of the club. Assume for a moment that the only part of the "perfect" golfer visible to the eye is the golfer's back elbow. If you were to stand directly on the target line behind that golfer, what do you think you'd notice about that visible elbow on every flawless swing? The golfer's back elbow would move from down (at address) to up (at the top of the backswing) to down (for impact with the ball) along a forty-five degree angle away from and back toward the target line.

FIGURE 5-1

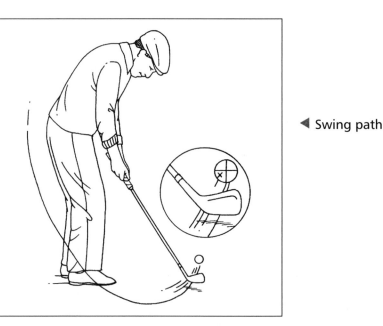

◀ Swing path

No body part can work alone. To keep the elbow on its proper path requires clearing the hips at the beginning of the downswing. Remember? The "cheeks" of your backside rolling on the wall clear the path for your back elbow to move unrestricted.

Swinging on Line

Swinging inside-out is swinging on line. Unfortunately, many golfers overthink the concept of club path and try to get the head of the club on line by guiding it toward the target line too early, thinking that by lining up the club head on the target path they'll hit straight shots. With the perfect swing, the club face will not be square to the target line and ready to strike the ball perfectly until impact with the ball. Any efforts to square the club face early or to get the club head on the target line will create unnecessary problems.

Yes, it's possible to do plenty of bad things in a swing and still hit the ball straight, but you'll lose power, or you'll hit the ball with power but send it off in the wrong direction. Take care not to overthink and not to "aim" the swing. Learn to swing inside-out and trust that your body, adapting to proper swing mechanics, will deliver consistent shots toward the target with good distance.

FACT

"On line" and "target line" are not the same. If you could take a string and attach it to the inside quarter of the ball on one end and to the butt of the club at the top of the backswing, then keep the butt of the club sliding straight down that string on the downswing, the swing would be "on line."

Swinging Outside-In

It's very difficult to hit accurate shots if your swing is typically an outside-in swing. Someone with this type of swing will either pull the ball (hit a straight shot far left of the target) or slice the ball (hit a ball that curves well to the right of the target). Of course, it's possible to hit thousands and thousands of practice shots and gain control over an outside-in swing, but any swing that's out of path lacks the power it ought to have.

To get an idea of what exactly an outside-in swing is, first address the ball. Now move the club off the target line and a smidgen toward your feet. This is considered "inside" the target line. Move the club to the other side of the target line, and this is considered "outside." An outside-in swing is a swing that makes contact with the ball as the club is moving on a path from outside the target line to inside the target line. An outside-in swing has one of two basic causes: one has to do with the shoulders, the other with the wrists. Once you recognize the root of the problem, work on that specific area until it becomes a natural part of your swing.

FACT

If you grew up playing several different sports and are now taking up the game, chances are good that you might begin playing golf with an outside-in swing. So much athletic motion in other sports—hitting a baseball, for example—requires horizontal movement of the shoulders and snap of the wrists for power. Both such actions virtually guarantee an outside-in swing.

Horizontal Movement of the Shoulders

Proper shoulder rotation, which in golf is more of a vertical rotation than a horizontal one, helps to keep the club on the proper path at every part of the swing. Draw that imaginary line from the target through the ball, and address the ball.

From the address position, pull your left shoulder back and your right shoulder forward along a horizontal plane two to four inches off parallel with the target line. Many golfers can draw the club back on the backswing close to the proper swing path, but those who try to generate power on the downswing by twisting their shoulders on this horizontal plane will strike the ball on an outside-in path. Draw the club to the top of your backswing, repeat that horizontal shoulder turn, and execute a downswing. See the swing path?

Early Release of the Wrists

Even very good, experienced golfers can develop outside-in swings, though usually not from the shoulders, but instead from the wrists. Specifically, these golfers often "release" the club too early in the swing—they allow their wrists to uncock—or try to make the swing more powerful by snapping their wrists as they would do when hitting a baseball.

To illustrate, draw the imaginary line from the target through the ball. Address the ball with your toes along another line parallel to the target line. Rotate the shoulders properly and bring the club to the top of the backswing. At this point, the club is pretty close to being parallel to the target line. Bring the club down until your hands are about hip high and the club is parallel to the ground and to the target line. As your hands slowly move toward striking the ball, the club head will slowly merge with the target line. At that point where the club is hip high and parallel both to the ground and to the target line, unhinge the wrists and watch what happens. The club head moves out so that now, as it approaches the ball, it is outside the target line, creating an outside-in swing.

FACT

Both accuracy and power in a golf swing come more from timing than from brute force. Brute force and poor timing cannot outdistance excellent timing alone. Whether you're physically strong or not, develop your timing on the golf swing first. Accuracy and distance will follow.

A Word about Shanks

When discussing swing paths, it's difficult to avoid mentioning shanks, even though most golfers will cringe at the word. The shanked shot is the most dreaded, and most dangerous, shot in golf.

A shank is the result of hitting the ball with the hosel instead of the club face. The hosel is the part of the club that attaches the club head to the shaft. If you've ever done this, you know that the ball can zoom off at about a ninety degree angle right of the target. But since the hosel is round, there really isn't any way to determine exactly where the ball will go. A person standing close by could very well get a face full of golf ball.

Why It Happens

A shanked shot is caused by an improper swing path. Address the ball and draw the backswing. As you bring the club back down toward impact, slowly push the club head away from your body, causing the heel of the club to veer off to the right of the target. Don't follow through, but stop the swing right before it impacts the ball. Notice the position of the club head in relation to the ball.

The club head will be to the right of the ball. Since you haven't moved from your position, the club must extend a bit in order to reach the other side of the ball. This creates a sharper angle of the club shaft. The sharper angle brings the hosel down slightly, causing it to connect with the ball. When the ball is struck with the hosel, it shoots off at a sharp angle (possibly injuring someone or ruining an otherwise well-played round of golf). Thus, the dreaded shank is born.

Correcting a Shank

If this is an all too familiar occurrence for you, don't despair. Nearly every golfer has experienced a shank or several during his or her golfing days. It can be corrected.

Get out a piece of plywood and set your ball on an imaginary line that runs from the target through your ball. Now create a line parallel to the target line approximately two inches away from the outside of the ball using cornstarch or talcum powder.

Address the ball and swing. If you hit the line of powder, you're likely to cause a shank. Now, address the ball again, and this time take only a half-swing, slow and controlled, concentrating on keeping your swing along the proper swing path to intersect the target line and force the club face to be square at impact. Read the section on the inside-out swing again and use it to visualize the proper swing path.

Repeat this drill over and over until you feel comfortable making the half-swing follow the proper swing path. Once you've mastered the half-swing, work on the full-swing. You're well on your way to eliminating shanks from your regular playing routine.

The Open Club Face

A golfer can have an excellent swing in terms of the club's path; however, if the club face is open (or closed) when the ball is struck, the ball will not go where the golfer planned for it to go. The club face is open when it's angled away from the golfer at address, and closed when it is angled toward the golfer.

What Causes an Open Club Face

Grip a club and address a ball. Pick a target line and line up. It may help to actually draw a target line on the ground. Position yourself properly and align the club face square to the target line. This is, of course, how we want the ball to be struck for a straight shot.

Study the line on your left hand between the forefinger knuckle and the knuckle of your pinkie. The two middle knuckles will bow out a bit, but the knuckles of your forefinger and pinkie will be on the same line as that square club face. (Okay, there's a tad of variance among golfers, but the club face and the knuckle line will be very close to identical.)

ALERT!

If you simply adapt your game to that "natural" swing you started off with, you'll never develop a better game. Accept the aggravation and learn to hit straight first. It will make you a vastly superior golfer over time.

Keep hold of the club and rotate the hands, tilting the knuckle line clockwise a little. Your pinkie knuckle is in front of the forefinger knuckle. Now, look at the club in relation to the ball. If your knuckles are in this position at impact, your club face will be open and you will impart a clockwise spin on the golf ball, causing the ball to curve to the right. The knuckles need to return to the start position at impact with the ball for the club face to be aligned square with the target line.

Your pinkie knuckle may be in front of the forefinger knuckle for one or both of these reasons: Your hands are releasing late, and/or at some point in your backswing you've given your hands a bit of a twist.

Open Club Face Pros and Cons

While an open club face does have its advantages, it's important to begin by thinking about the negatives of an open club face since the first goal for any golfer should be to learn to swing the club properly and to hit straight shots. Everything else about golf is dependent upon that solid, basic swing.

An open club face can:

- Reduce the distance a golf shot is supposed to travel.
- Cause the ball to curve away from the target line.
- Cut the roll of the ball after it lands.

You will become a much better golfer if you master all the mechanics for straight golf shots first. After all, you'll never hear any golfer complain that all of his or her shots go straight down the target line.

FIGURE 5-2

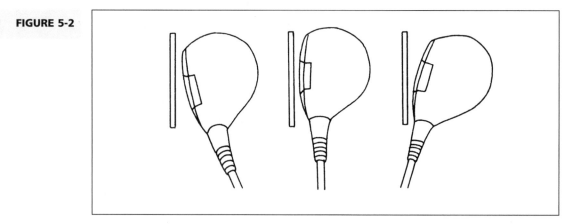

▲ Club faces: closed, square, and open

On the other hand, an open club face is useful when you decide it's to your advantage on certain shots. Leaving out the uses of an open face for finesse around the greens, the values of being able to use an open club face include:

- Playing a golf shot around trouble.
- Holding the target line in a crosswind.
- Reducing the roll of the ball after it lands.

The Closed Club Face

If the forefinger knuckle of your left hand is millimeters closer to the target than the knuckle of your pinkie at impact with the ball, the club face will be closed. (A closed club face is angled toward the golfer.) Assuming that the swing path is correct, a closed club face striking the golf ball will impart a counterclockwise spin and the ball will curve to the left. Again, you want the knuckles of your forefinger and pinkie to be on the same line as that square club face at impact with the ball if you want to hit a straight shot.

Causes of a Closed Club Face

There is one primary cause a club could be closed at impact: Your hands are releasing the club too soon. You can simulate this problem by addressing the ball in the proper position and then bending your left wrist, making it concave, so that the back of your hand is closer to your forearm.

Closed Club Face Pros and Cons

Once again, the minuses are put first to emphasize that every golfer who wants to improve is better off focusing on developing an excellent swing motion that produces straight shots before surrendering to a "natural" hook.

A closed club face can:

- Roll farther on the ground and into trouble.
- Curve away from the target line.

FACT

The best golfers make very subtle changes to create the desired spins on the ball. They do not exaggerate the club face angle.

On the other hand, a shot planned to take advantage of a closed club face can improve your golf game by:

- Playing around trouble.
- Helping the shot hold with the target line in a crosswind.

The Square Club Face

If an open club face sends the ball slicing (curving) to the right of the target line, and a closed club face sends the ball hooking (curving) to the left of the target line, then a square club face will send the ball along the target line. This is assuming, of course, that your swing is on path, that you are lined up properly, and that the basic swing motion has engaged all the parts of the body with the right timing.

If, when you address the ball, the club face is square to the target line and the knuckles of your forefinger and pinkie on your left hand are also square to the target line, then the properly executed swing will return the club face and the knuckles to that setup position, and the ball will fly true to course.

ALERT!

If you have to make adjustments to the angle of the club face at setup in order to hit the ball straight, something's wrong with your swing. The ball may go straight after the adjustment, but you'll never be able to hit is as accurately, as far, or with the right spin.

Combining Swing Path and Face Angle

You've learned about swing path and club face angle as though they impact the golf ball separately. Of course, they don't. It is the club face that strikes the ball, the shaft that propels the club head, and the swing that powers the shaft—meaning, a combination of factors affect the flight of the ball.

You should spend ample time making certain the ingredients of a good swing come together. Ben Hogan once said: "I see no reason, truly, why the average golfer, if he goes about it intelligently, shouldn't play in the 70s—and I mean by playing the type of shots a fine golfer plays." (in *Five Lessons: The Modern Fundamentals of Golf*, 1985, by Ben Hogan)

Following is a chart of the deflections affecting ball flight. Logically, it's easier to eliminate all the wrong things one by one than to create ways around them. Ⓔ

FIGURE 5-3

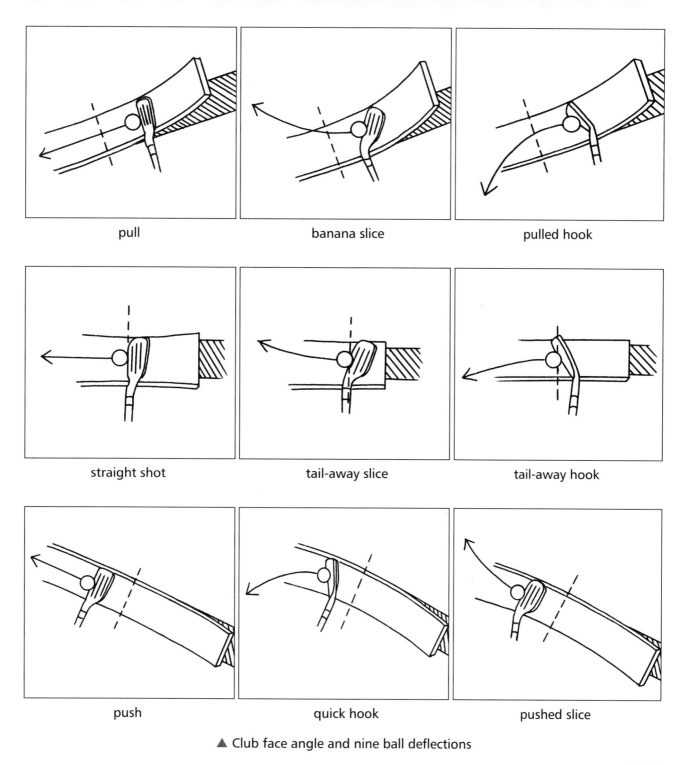

pull

banana slice

pulled hook

straight shot

tail-away slice

tail-away hook

push

quick hook

pushed slice

▲ Club face angle and nine ball deflections

Chapter 6

Swinging with Power

Have you ever watched a golfer send a missile off the tee and heard the sound of the shaft of the club whistling through the air as you stood by in awe? Well, now it's your turn to learn how to let loose the power. This chapter will show you how to build the momentum needed for a powerful swing.

Start with Balance

Pick a sport, any sport, and balance is always a key ingredient. Balance yields stability, and stability allows you to repeat the same motion—in this case, the golf swing—over and over. But stability does not necessarily yield power. The right balance is both stable and powerful.

A Balanced and Power Stance

By now it's obvious to you that a golf swing requires a lot of motion from the whole body, but especially the upper body. Your stance has to keep all that movement balanced—all that movement swinging together for perfect contact, for powerful contact. At the same time, if you're too focused on stability, you may develop a stance that is very stable, but that hinders the proper motion a good swing is supposed to generate.

For points of reference, use the instep of both feet and your shoulders, both where your shoulders join with the torso and the outside point of your shoulders. First, line up the insteps of your feet with your shoulders' torso connection and take a practice swing. There's a good possibility that somewhere near the top of the backswing, or near the swing's low point, or on the follow-through (or maybe all three) you had to struggle to maintain balance. Your feet were probably going through countless tiny corrections to keep you in balance.

FACT

A good stance will not only maintain your balance, but also help your basic swing motion. With a stance too narrow or too wide, your body's contribution to the swing is limited. With a good, comfortable stance, your body is allowed the room it needs to rotate around the fixed axis and generate power, while supporting the proper weight shifts.

Now, place your feet wider, with the insteps aligned with the points of your shoulders. This is actually the correct position, so just for fun, add the width of each foot to the width of that stance. Now take a practice swing. You might find that your weight stays somewhere between both feet throughout your swing, but you still feel something isn't just right. If so, you probably strained and failed to rotate your hips and shoulders as far as you could with the very narrow stance.

This time align your insteps with your shoulder cups and swing. This is the position of harmony between flexibility and stability.

The Athletic Position

You have a definite picture in your mind of "the athletic position" if you've been involved in sports throughout your life. Certainly different sports require different movements, but the athletic position summons the image of someone "ready." This person has his or her weight centered near the balls of the feet, knees slightly flexed, and a bit of bend at the waist. If you're having trouble picturing this, think of a soccer goalie, an infielder, a cornerback in football, a tennis player ready to receive a 130-mile-an-hour serve, a basketball player playing defense, and now, a golfer preparing to strike the ball.

Some golfers have a tendency to bend too much at the knees. Too much bend limits the swing in a way that is similar to a stance that is too wide. It also flattens the lie of the club, making the swing less vertical and more horizontal, which makes the likelihood of pulls and slices much greater.

Another common problem is to stand with knees almost unbent, which causes the golfer to tilt more from the waist. This also reduces the use of the lower body to help generate power in the swing. With the knees properly flexed, the entire body falls into the athletic position and contributes to the swing.

ALERT!

Your athletic position won't be identical to someone else's, so don't try to imitate perfectly your golfing partner. If you're quite tall, it's likely you'll need to bend a little more at the waist than your shorter friend. That's perfectly fine. Find the stance and athletic position that's comfortable, balanced, and suited to your physique.

Motion of the Hands

The swing, the rhythm, the turn with shoulder and hip rotation, and all the body's muscles come together to compose a physical symphony of two notes: whir and whack. The power of your swing comes from the speed of the club head at impact. Though your hands are certainly important (you have to hold the club somehow), never think that you swing with your hands.

The hands grip the club. They grip it tight enough so that the club will not slip. They grip it loose enough so that the muscles of the arms are not restricted in the movement along the swing path. Some may argue that the hands begin the backswing, pulling the club away from the ball at address, but the hands don't initiate the downswing, and they're not part of the club acceleration until just before the moment of impact. Never, never swing with your hands.

Muscle Coil

Muscle coil is an image and a feel, not a physiological occurrence, because muscles don't coil; they work in antagonistic pairs. However, this image and feel may be of help to you when trying to understand how the muscles behave to strike the ball powerfully. Think of the energy stored in a watch spring when wound. The coil tightens around a fixed axis. Once wound, it releases its energy as it uncoils.

Muscles don't actually coil. They alternately stretch and contract to create every movement of the body. Still, "coil" is a good image to describe the feeling of contraction and tightness as the swing (winding the clock) approaches the peak of the backswing and begins converting that wound-up energy into power.

Swinging for power demands that the muscles of your body alternately contract and stretch around your spine. To understand the coiled feel, think of dividing the body into thirds: lower body, torso, and arms.

Coil in the Lower Body

The bones and muscles of the lower body twist the hips forty-five degrees away from the target line. As the swing winds up (storing energy for the downswing), the hips turn and the weight shifts until, at the top of the backswing, the golfer should feel stretch along the inside of the front leg, stretch along the outside of the back leg, and contraction in the buttocks. At the finish of the follow-through, the golfer should feel stretch along the inside of the back leg, stretch along the outside of the front leg, and contraction in the buttocks.

Coil in the Torso and Arms

The torso helps twist the hips forty-five degrees from the target line and the shoulders another forty-five degrees beyond the hips. At the top of the coil, the golfer should feel stretch along the front side including the length of the front arm, mostly in the triceps but in the forearm, too. At the finish, the stretch settles to the side and the back arm.

Added to the process, the deltoids are busy raising the arms, while the latissimus dorsi muscles are busy helping to turn the shoulders from the hips another forty-five degrees. Those back muscles also help to pull the arms down as the shoulders stretch. When the arm bends at the elbow, the biceps muscle contracts and the triceps stretches, while at impact, the biceps stretches and the triceps contracts.

FACT

Strong, flexible muscles improve the power of your swing. Good news! Studies show that anyone of any age in reasonable health can dramatically improve muscular strength and flexibility with regular exercise. That's another way of saying if you aren't gaining yards, you probably aren't training your muscles.

Turning Speed

Turning speed is created by the initial thrust of the lower body: the push off your back foot and the turn of your front hip, all controlled by your legs, which have the largest muscles in your body. You may remember that Nolan Ryan (all-time strikeout king) pitched into his mid-forties, still throwing a fastball almost 100 miles an hour. People in the know said it was because of how well he used his legs. In golf, the power and efficiency of the initial thrust of your lower body establishes the maximum power your swing can generate.

Think of the turning speed you can build with your body in terms of the *Saturn 5* rocket which sent astronauts to the moon. The first stage, while the rocket is still on the ground, contains the most thrust. Though it travels the least distance and may not seem to move the rocket very fast, it initiates all the necessary movement to send the spaceship to the moon. Similarly, your feet won't move much, except to rock, but the back foot push establishes your maximum thrust.

The second stage of the rocket travels farther and faster than the first, but its speed is directly related to the power of stage one. Stage two would be the hip stage for a golfer. The third stage is again farther and faster than the previous stage, but power and speed are contingent upon the power and speed of stage two. This third stage is the torso and shoulder stage for the golfer. The final stage is much faster and travels much farther than any other stage, but contributes less to the overall power. This stage utilizes the golfer's arms and hands.

Study golfers on the practice tee. The best golfers with the most distance on their shots will seem to swing slowest; the not-so-good golfers will look more like they are swatting at hornets. Turning speed and power begin in the legs.

QUESTION?

What does *loft* mean?
It all depends on how you use the word. "Loft" can refer to the slant on the face of a club; to the angle of the club face in relation to the ground; and to the act of hitting the ball in the air, that is, to loft the ball.

Club Face Angle and Power Loss

You've read about club face angle and power in an earlier chapter, where the emphasis was on learning to make the club strike the ball properly. There are two differing club face angles to keep in mind. The first one has already been discussed at length—namely, the position of the club face relative to the target line. A club face perpendicular to the target line will transfer the most power of every club from the swing to the ball. The second angle is loft (angle of the club face in relation to the ground), which determines how high and on what angle the ball will be launched into the sky, and with what amount of spin. Greater loft means higher flight, less distance, and more backspin.

There is, however, another component to the angle of flight of the ball off the ground and the subsequent carry: the low point of the swing. If the low point of the swing comes at or slightly in front of the ball, you maximize both the spin and the distance for that club. If the low point comes just barely behind the ball and the club begins the upswing, loft is increased along with spin, and distance is decreased.

FIGURE 6-1

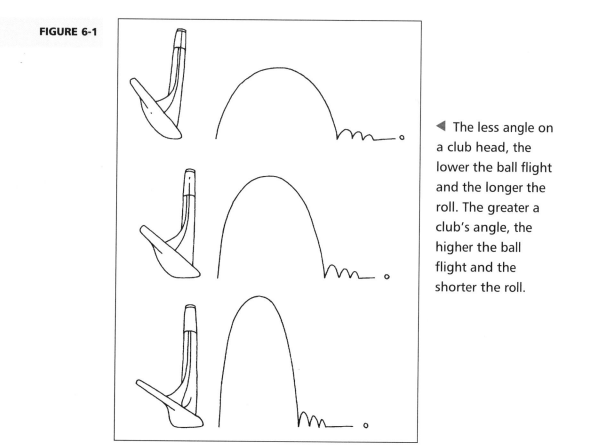

◀ The less angle on a club head, the lower the ball flight and the longer the roll. The greater a club's angle, the higher the ball flight and the shorter the roll.

Effective Loft

The loft of the club is affected by the designed angle on the face of the club and by the angle of the club to the ground at impact. While there are certain situations in which a golfer may want to increase the loft by "laying back" the club face (opening the club face) or decrease the loft by "hooding" the club (keeping the hands far forward of the ball on the ground), the best way to learn to play with your clubs is to first learn to take maximum advantage of what the loft of each club is designed to do for that club.

One good goal for the beginner is to learn to generate as much power with the swing as possible and employ it as accurately as possible. Longer distance off the tee increases your ability to put the ball closer to the pin on the green by allowing you to use more-lofted clubs to aim for the pin (or the right target on the green).

The Value of the Lower Lofted Clubs

The drivers in most beginner sets of clubs have a loft of twelve degrees. While this design is intended to help the beginner get the drive into the air, twelve degrees is not much loft. The driver is intended to hit the ball further than any other club in the bag and with more roll once it hits the ground. The higher the number of the club, the greater the loft, the shorter the carry (the distance the ball will travel in the air), and the quicker the stop once the ball is on the ground.

ALERT!

A golfer going for the green of a par five in two may use a lower lofted club to get the carry and the roll needed to get the ball close to the flag. The disadvantage is that sometimes the golfer will roll that shot into trouble. Other times a golfer will lay up short of the green and plan a third shot with a wedge, knowing that the wedge will get the ball close.

The Value of the Higher Lofted Clubs

The pitching wedge is intended to toss the ball high into the air and flop the ball down onto the green. If you're further away from the green than a couple dozen yards, say 75 to 100 yards away, that pitching wedge will toss the ball high, spin the ball, and cause it to stop dead on the green or back up. The advantage of higher lofted clubs—wedges, nine irons, and on down toward the lower numbers—is control of the ball in shorter yardage situations.

Whip Cracking—The Braking Mechanism

Some teaching pros never mention this whip-cracking phenomenon. They either don't believe it happens, or they believe it will confuse a golfer. Other pros swear by it. They believe it happens at the instant before and during contact with the ball. They believe it's the action that causes the best golfers in the world to launch rockets off the tee. In the terms of physics, whip cracking is called "angular momentum."

Angular Momentum at Work

If you ever cracked a whip, you've seen angular momentum at work. Or, if you fly fish, the same principle is operative. At the end of the forward wrist action, the whip and the fishing line sail forward at an accelerated speed far greater than the speed of the wrist.

FACT

A "Texas wedge" is a putter used from well off the green. If the hole is flat and there are no bunkers protecting the hole, golfers will hit the putter firmly, skittering the ball toward the green: no loft, longer roll, and less control. Learn to hit your wedge, and increase accuracy and lower your score.

How It Works in the Golf Swing

After you master the basic swing motion, the whip-cracking phenomenon happens effortlessly. As you swing, you bump your hips forward, begin your body rotation and the downswing, and your entire body rapidly generates more and more club-head speed with each passing instant. Your hands are moving fastest as they approach the low point of your swing travel. Then, as your body turns toward the finish, your hands begin a rapid deceleration, just like the end of a fly fishing motion. It's at this instant when your hands have completed their acceleration and begun the deceleration that angular momentum releases your wrists, delivering a club-head strike of the ball at a speed dramatically faster than your hands could possibly travel.

Study on the Range

Now that you understand angular momentum, study a few golfers on the range. You'll notice some golfers who seem to take mighty swats at the ball, yet their golf balls don't travel any remarkable distance despite the expenditure of energy. Then you see other golfers, whose swings seem slow, perhaps extremely slow. Yet, just prior to the "click" when club meets ball, you hear the whirring sound as the shaft and club head scream through the air. The swing is slow and effortless, but the club head is fast.

The first golfer is trying to muscle the ball by snapping his wrists early, thinking that he is generating power. The second golfer is taking advantage of angular momentum, keeping his wrists cocked until nearly the end of the downstroke.

When to Unleash

How do you know when to release the wrists to unleash this lightening bolt in your stroke? There are two answers really. The first one is practice, practice, practice. The second answer is more controversial, but it does have a growing number of proponents: Don't think about it. When turning through the basic motion properly, as your hands reach that point of rapid deceleration, your cocked wrists simply can't contain the angular momentum and they release automatically at the right time.

Chapter 7

Keeping Your Swing Consistent

It's not a good idea to pick out a favorite golfer and attempt to copy that golfer's swing. It might work if you're the same height and your bodies are proportioned exactly the same. But in reality, different builds call for different swings. The key to a good swing is the same for you as for every golfer: consistency.

Shoulder Tilt

The club you put in your hands dictates the distance you stand from the ball. There's a different distance for each club. In the same way, your height, the length of your legs, and the length of your back combine to dictate your proper shoulder tilt. Generally speaking, the taller your are, the more your shoulders will tilt toward vertical; the shorter you are, the less vertical the tilt.

On Their Own Plane

It once was thought that the hands and the shoulders traveled along the same plane during the swing. However, high-speed cameras have demonstrated the folly of that approach. The shoulders and the hands travel on their own respective planes, and each plane is parallel to the target line.

Indulge in this extreme hypothetical situation for a moment. If the ball rested on a tee that elevated the ball all the way up to shoulder height, then arguably the hands and shoulders would be on the same horizontal plane. But the closer the ball is played toward the feet (the shorter the club), the more those planes will differ.

Given the athletic flex in the lower body, the tilt at the waist, and the tilt of the torso to forty-five degrees, the shoulders must find the path that fits the club with the properly positioned body. Keeping the fixed axis of the spine in mind, the shoulders should maintain their own plane parallel to the target line during the swing.

Imagine a golfer wearing a sheet of plywood with a hole cut out for his or her head, the board resting atop the shoulders. Part of the sheet of plywood extends beyond the back of the golfer's head. Another piece of plywood rests on the ground on the target line. Assuming you could swing a club wearing this contraption, your hands would remain behind this plywood (shoulder plane) near the bottom of the swing and cross it at the top of the swing. As you can see, shoulders and hands work together, but they travel in their own planes parallel to the target line.

Never Chase the Shoulder Tilt

The golf swing begins from the ground up. Put the body in an athletic position with knees and ankles flexed, and the proper body tilts. The adaptation for your shoulders is really minimal. The club has already dictated the distance from the ball. Simply let your shoulders go along for the ride. Let the club and your body build determine the right shoulder tilt.

ALERT!

Some golfers attempt to swing with an identical club angle for each shot, moving in and out from the ball, and standing with legs straighter or more bent at the knees. Don't change your swing for every club. Let the club fit your swing. Shoulder tilt differences will be minimal.

Left Arm Turn

The turn of the left arm begins with the movement of the shoulders. Nothing about the swing operates independently of any other part. The shoulders move the arms and the club at the start. The left arm (front arm) has two roles as it moves through the swing path. It helps keep the shaft of the club aligned at the target line, and it helps the left hand to rotate properly.

Left Arm, Club Shaft, and Target Line

As the shoulders turn, which in doing so turn the left arm, the club comes away from the address position. When the club is pulled away so that the head of the club is just about hip high and the shaft of the club is parallel to the ground, the left arm should have aligned the club so that it is on a line parallel to the target line and parallel to the ground.

At the top of the backswing, the shaft of the club should be parallel to the target line again. For many good golfers, the left arm keeps the club on a parallel line from the time the club head is hip high all the way through the backswing. Consider your left arm your guide arm, keeping the club properly aligned in reference to the target along the swing path.

Left Arm and the Back of the Left Hand

The back of your left hand should be vertical (aligned with the club face) at address. It should be flat to the path of the club at the top of the backswing, return to vertical at impact, and face the sky in the follow-through.

Pretend you're addressing the ball with the club gripped only in your left hand. Open your hand so that your fingers point toward the ball. The back of your hand should be aligned square to the target line, on a vertical plane. Now sweep the left hand along the path of the backswing. At the top of the backswing, the back of your left hand stays aligned with the face of the club, allowing your left arm to move naturally along the swing path and rotate as it's designed to do.

Bring your hands back down toward impact. Your left arm should rotate your left hand so that it's once more square to the ball. Bring the hand on through the follow-through. Notice the natural rotation. This natural rotation will help keep your swing consistent.

Sometimes it's difficult to both watch what you're doing and concentrate on what you should be doing. In which case, you may find it helpful to use a friend or a video camera. A friend will be able to tell you what you're doing when you do it, but a video can be watched several times over as you analyze and re-analyze your address and swing.

Left Arm Alignment

One of the first pieces of advice you're likely to hear as a beginner is to keep your left arm straight. The advice is dead on the money, but not in an absolutely literal sense.

It's true the straight left arm keeps the club and hands properly on path, and if the left elbow bends significantly prior to impact, ball flight will be erratic. But a beginner concentrating on a straight left arm—locking the elbow in a effort to keep it stiff—will dramatically reduce the power and the ease of the swing. Stand in front of a mirror with your eyes closed and straighten your left arm in a comfortable way, then take a look. The arm is "straight," but it's not a perfect 180 degrees from biceps to wrist. It's more in the neighborhood of 175 to 178 degrees. Maintain that comfortable "straight" position, and your arms and hands will be able to swing freely, easily, and powerfully.

Right Elbow Tuck

While it's your left arm that does most of the work—staying straight to guide the club and hands along the swing path—don't overlook the worth of the right arm . . . or rather, the right elbow. The proper motion of the right elbow is of the utmost importance to uncoiling the backswing and maintaining the proper swing path. Take a look at some of the golfers at the range or on the course. Notice anything similar in the position of their right elbows at the top of their backswings? Hopefully, they all have the right elbow tucked in toward their body.

Now, it's your turn. Address the ball and take a backswing, stopping at the top of the backswing. Where is your right elbow? Is it sticking out away from your body, or is it tucked in toward your body? If the back elbow sticks out away from the body at the top of the backswing, you're likely to pull or slice the ball. If you keep it tucked in toward the body, you're much more likely to bring the club down the proper swing path to make solid contact with the ball. Also keep in mind that from address through impact, the right and left elbows should remain the same distance apart.

Myths about Weight Shift

Often the word "myth" is used to mean falsehoods, but there's another definition. Myth means sacred story or explanation that illuminates truth deeper than what is seen in the material world. There are two basic myths about weight shift: Weight shift begins the swing, and the swing initiates weight shift. Excellent teachers of the game can be found supporting each.

The First Myth

Proponents of the myth that weight shift begins the swing start their argument with the legs. The swing begins from the ground up. So, the hips and torso can begin their turn only after the weight begins to shift from centered between the legs toward the back leg. In other words, the beginning of the weight shift makes possible the turn of the hips and the torso around the fixed axis. The weight shift then leads the body toward the top of the backswing where the weight will be centered along the inside of the right leg and away from the left leg. Next, the shift of the weight forward helps the hips to move forward and twist to the left. It's the shift of the weight off the right leg and back onto the left that initiates the powerful downward motion of the swing.

ALERT!

It's important that your body doesn't sway as you shift your weight. Though your body parts will be moving to create the basic swing motion, the weight shift is subtle. If your body sways, you may tip or even fall over, not to mention produce a faulty swing path.

The Second Myth

Proponents of the myth that the swing begins the weight shift may point to the greater flexibility of the torso and the arms, and the need of torso and arms to rotate further and faster and to unwind further and faster after the top of the backswing. Since the torso and arms travel further and faster, it is this part of the body—the actual swing portion of the movement—that initiates the shift in weight. Movement first, weight shift second.

Truths about Weight Shift and Balance

Which side of the weight shift debate do you lean toward? The debate about weight shift can be recast into some absolute truths regardless of the weight shift myth you believe in.

The Athletic Position Maintains Balance

Too much focus on shifting the weight will cause the beginner to pull the upper body off the swing path. Camp out at any golf course for half a day and you'll see the awkward gyrations some golfers go through to shift their weight the way they think they're supposed to. Some of them have to fight to recover from the weight shift so they don't fall over.

Think back to the athletic position common to many sports: legs flexed, torso tilted, weight centered, and body ready for action. Envision a base runner in the big leagues preparing to steal second base. The pitcher eyes him, and the base runner gets his lead and stares back. If the pitcher throws to home plate, the base runner will race to second. Slowly the base runner shifts his weight toward the leg closest to second base. Suddenly the pitcher throws to first. Great base runners, despite the weight shift toward second base, are still balanced enough to make the quick lunge safely back to first base. The athletic position should control the amount of weight shift, keeping the athlete (you the golfer) on balance throughout the swing.

Correct balance and weight shift aren't very easy to explain in words—they must be felt to be understood. To make the most of the sections on balance and weight shift, put the book aside for a moment, stand up, and try it out for yourself. It will help even more if you practice with a golf club. Soon you'll get the feel of good balance and proper weight shift.

The Hips Never Cross the Line

Balance, balance, balance. When discussing any part of the golf swing, balance can never be overstated. If you've just taken a mighty swing at the golf ball and you didn't fall backward, it means you didn't leave your weight over your back leg. If you didn't fall toward the target, then you didn't thrust your weight too far forward. But you could still be falling off balance toward your toes, or need a little jab step backward to keep from falling over your heels. If you must correct for balance in any direction, your swing doesn't carry the punch your body generated when you coiled. Worse still, your shot may not go in the direction intended because your balance problems may have shifted the path of the club.

If you're falling either toward the ball's position on the ground or directly away, the rotation of your hips is likely to blame. At address, your hips are parallel to the target line. Draw an imaginary line across your hips at address and do not cross it. As your hips initiate the downswing— beginning the forward weight shift and the hips' rotation to clear the way for your arms and hands—they should never cross that line. Your back hip on its rotation may touch the line, but crossing the line will draw the swing out of path. Neither should your back hip fall away from the line on the downswing and follow-through.

The Greatest Weight Balance Truth of All

Good weight shift and balance occurs almost naturally in those who have mastered the basic swing motion. To concentrate your efforts on weight shift is to concentrate on the wrong part of the swing. If you drill adequately on the fundamentals of the swing, you'll know when your balance isn't in sync and modest mental corrections will pull your balance in line.

FACT

Another fundamental truth is that practice makes perfect—well, nearly perfect. A consistent swing requires lots and lots of practice. Don't expect to hit a few balls and have it down pat. If golf were that easy, it wouldn't be much of a challenge, nor would it be much fun.

The Tilt

A consistent swing requires the torso to remain at a nearly constant tilt throughout the backswing. But don't misinterpret this. The tilt is not constant, only nearly so.

One of the authors of this book, with the aid of a builder, constructed a teaching tool from a steel pipe to simulate the tilt. In strapping the shoulders to a device that allowed a student to swing freely through a full range of motion on the swing path, it was found that the tilt is constant on a half swing, from back to forward. However, when the club is raised toward a full backswing or a full follow-through, the spine tilts several degrees behind and forward. The tilt of the spine is only *nearly* constant.

Losing Consistency

Many golfers lose consistency to the swing when they allow the tilt to increase on the backswing. As the left shoulder drops and the right shoulder raises on the backswing, some tend to increase the tilt of the torso, bending further at the waist. Or, they shift the tilt toward the back foot thinking it has something to do with proper weight shift. On the downswing, some raise the torso in a mistaken effort to lift the ball; others rock the axis forward, again thinking about weight shift.

Think of It as Constant

It's probably best to lock the tilt in your mind as a constant, but close examination with fast film suggests that were the tilt rigidly constant, the shoulders would not be able to complete the turn to ninety degrees at the top of the backswing, nor finish completely in the follow-through. Keeping the tilt (nearly) constant helps the golfer maintain the low point of the swing and achieve consistent ball striking.

FACT

Pitchers throw curve balls to keep the baseball from maintaining a constant position in relation to a batter's horizontal, fixed swing axis. When a golfer changes the tilt during the swing, in effect, the golfer is tossing him- or herself curve balls.

The Finish

One way to tell how well you've hit the ball is how you finish. However, keep in mind that it's possible to hit the ball toward your intended target while doing several things wrong with your swing. A misaligned club combined with a poor swing path may permit you to hit a golf ball straight, but you've robbed yourself of power, consistency, and the ability to diagnose what has gone wrong when your game goes belly up. That's just another way of saying that the shot isn't over when the club hits the ball.

When all the ingredients of a good swing motion are in place, you'll know that you're making good shots and repeating them over and over by the way your body and club finish. Here are some key ingredients to the finish:

- Your belly button is turned toward the target or parallel to the target line.
- Your back shoulder is pointed at the target.
- Your weight is centered over your front foot with your front leg straight.
- Your back knee has turned and almost touches your front knee.

To finish in these great positions might mean nothing—it's possible to concentrate so much on the finish that, just as could happen with a really poor swing, you could put together enough errant ingredients so that your body winds up with all these checkpoints.

Don't focus on the finish; let the finish be a diagnostic tool. Take some swings, hit some practice balls, and check for the points of a great finish. A consistent swing around a fixed axis using all the right ingredients you have learned will deliver your body to these alignments. (E)

Chapter 8
Shot Making

Shot making is not giving the ball a whack off the tee and having it land down the fairway on the line you intended. That's a good shot, but it isn't shot making. Shot making has to do with controlling the ball, having it curve when it needs to or backing it up on the green when necessary.

Footwork

The feet are the least active parts of the body during the swing, but they're active. Good shot-making ability demands that a golfer keep the swing fluid—never jerky, never changing rhythm in an effort to change the flight of the ball. In order to do this, a golfer must know what to do with the feet.

The Front Foot

In an earlier era of golf instruction, some teachers taught that the heel of the front foot lifted off the ground during the backswing and was to be stomped to the ground at the initial stage of the downswing. It was thought that this helped to create a smoother swing. Although some golfers mastered this technique, for most it created shifts in the body position during the swing and increased the potential for a jerky, less consistent motion on the downswing.

Today's teachers would never suggest a raised front heel, but part of the turn on the backswing does include the "roll" of the front ankle slightly toward the ground. The roll inward toward the ground of the front ankle helps with the smooth shifting of the weight toward the back foot.

The Back Foot

On the downswing, the back foot does two things. First, following the lead of the hips moving forward and rotating, the ankle of the back foot rolls toward the ground, smoothing the shift of weight toward the front foot. Second, because of the acceleration of the downswing, the weight shift does not occur as rapidly, thus generating momentum and mass along the back leg, causing the back heel to lift from the ground.

E ALERT!

If the heel comes off the ground too early, the hips will turn out toward the ball. This will cause the club to get out of path.

As the back ankle rolls, the foot pushes, at first, from heel to toe, driving the accelerating swing and the uncoiling body along the spinal axis. The further the swing moves toward impact, the more the pushing action shifts from the whole foot and toward the ball of the foot until the heel of the back foot raises from the ground.

Wrists and Club Face Angle

You'll find some disagreement among golf instructors about how quickly the wrists should bend, or cock, on the backswing. There are countless examples of good golfers who do it differently, so there really isn't any one right way. However, there's almost complete unanimity on at least three things having to do with the wrists: Uncocking the wrists during the downswing, and cupping or bowing the wrists during backswing will all keep you off target.

Uncock Your Wrists Later

To achieve maximum club-head speed, your wrists must release, and this occurs almost naturally. But for many who grew up playing baseball, the wrists will probably tend to release too early. As mentioned before, this will throw the club outside the path. It also decreases club-head speed, causing loss of power, and prevents the ball from traveling toward the target.

FACT

If you're getting all the other ingredients of the swing right—the feet, hips, and so on—the speed you generate with the club head will just about release that club head for you at the right time.

Have you ever been on the practice tee hitting balls and suddenly out of nowhere you launched the ball twenty yards farther than you usually do, and with great ease? You probably spent the rest of the session trying to figure out what you did right. Well, there's a good chance you released the club later than you usually do.

Avoid the Cupped Wrist in the Backswing

A cupped left wrist in the backswing will cause the club face to be open at impact. Grip an imaginary club and cock your wrists as you normally would by the top of your backswing. If the knuckles of your left wrist are drawn toward your left forearm, then your wrist cupped. This means that the club face is open, and you're going to hit a ball that will curve to the right of the target line as it moves toward the target.

Avoid the Bowed Wrist in the Backswing

Take the imaginary club and cock the wrists again. If the knuckles pull away from the forearm, you're going to hit the ball to the left of target line. Also, the ball will have plenty of roll, probably enough roll to get you into even more trouble.

ESSENTIAL

Learning to play different shots—draws and fades, cuts and knockdowns—effectively requires mastery of the basic swing motion, being able to hit the ball the direction you want it to go consistently. Only then are you ready to make the minor adjustments necessary to shape different shots.

Learning to Draw the Ball

Many golfers agree that in order to draw and fade a ball, you have to just think about it. Well, it takes a little more than that, but not much. After you master the basic swing motion, your body will make the subtle adjustments needed and you'll scarcely be aware of it. Practice enough and see if that doesn't become true for you. However, in the meantime, there are some things you'll need to know.

First, the definition: A draw is a shot that curves from the right of the target line to the left toward the target. That's a good definition to remember because it tells you how to set up to play a draw.

While it may seem as though drawing the ball is the same as hooking the ball, there's one big difference. Drawing the ball is an intentional shot meant to follow the curve of the hole. A hook is not under the golfer's control and usually causes the ball to curve sharply to the left. It's all about control. Don't think that if you have a problem hooking, you can brag about your drawing skills to your golf buddies. They may just put you to the test!

Alignment for a Draw

Align your club on the target line. Nothing unusual here. Sounds just like what you've already learned, doesn't it? Do this exactly as if you were going to hit a straight shot. Stand behind the ball, pick the target in the distance, pick an intermediate target three to six feet in front of the ball, and align the club face square to the target line.

Next, align your stance slightly to the right. Pick a target several degrees to the right of your target and place your feet on a line parallel to that target line. You're only looking for a few degrees, perhaps five to fifteen degrees. Then, deploy your basic swing motion and—eureka!—a draw! Well, maybe not the very first time, but you get the idea. Keep practicing and soon you'll draw a ball as though you've been doing it all your life.

Cautions

Your body and brain may try to compensate for the minor shift in your stance. This could cause you to change your swing enough to hit toward the original target line. It could also cause you to adjust the club head on the downswing, which may make you hit to the right of your real target. Don't readjust your club head, and don't exaggerate your stance further to the right. Practice, practice, practice.

FACT

Many gifted golfers find that the basic swing motion gives them a natural draw to begin with. No problems here. If you discover this is true for you, make the minor adjustments necessary to cause the ball to fly toward the target line, and enjoy the extra roll that draws ordinarily get.

Learning to Fade the Ball

A shot that fades starts left of the target line and curves to the right toward the target line. Don't confuse this with a slice. A fade is an intentional shot made to follow the curve of the hole. A fade is under the golfer's control, a slice is not.

A slice curves way right of the target line. A lot of beginners have trouble with a slice. In fact, it's been estimated that 80 percent of all golfers, beginners and otherwise, always have trouble with a slice. If that's your problem, you may just want to stick with the basic swing motion and learn to hit the ball straight. On the other hand, understanding how to work a fade may help you correct your slicing problem.

Alignment for a Fade

This is just like the draw, only in reverse. Position your club face square to the target line, just as you would for a straight shot. Then align your stance slightly to the left. Pick a target a few degrees to the left of the real target and align your body from the feet through the knees, hips, and shoulders on lines parallel to that new target. Swing for the new target.

What Happens

The ball will leave the ground (or the tee) on the new target line, left of the true target line. Then the clockwise spin on the ball will send the ball curving right. (Of course, this assumes that your brain doesn't recoordinate your body so that it hits the ball straight.) Fades tend to travel less distance after landing than do draws because the spin imparted is more directly sidespin.

Fades and draws require a lot of practice. Though it's easy to tell you to align your stance slightly to the left or to the right, you aren't really going to know how far to the left or right you should turn until you get out there and try it out. Since not every hole will have the same curve, you need to learn to adjust your stance to fit the curve of the hole.

ESSENTIAL

Learning to make the ball go straight first will help you to be more successful in learning to make the ball curve. Feet, knees, hips, and shoulders are all on their own lines parallel to the target line. Your most important shot-making tip is to hit straight shots with the proper parallel alignments first. Then, controlling the ball—drawing, fading, and cutting—will be much easier to master.

Using Backspin

It will always be difficult to impossible to land a one iron on the green and make it stop dead or back up. Likewise it will be difficult to impossible to hit a wedge (unless you top it) and send it rolling yards and yards onward after it touches the ground. Every golfer is always better off using each club in the bag as it's designed to be used. Irons eight and nine, and the wedges sand and pitching, readily put backspin on a ball when well struck.

To increase the backspin on a ball, decrease the tilt of the spine. If you stand up straighter when addressing the ball, you'll swing on a steeper angle. A steeper angle of the club will increase backspin. If your local club uses rye grass on its fairways, a beginner will have a tougher time getting the lofted clubs to spin the ball backward. On the other hand, if your local course uses Bermuda or zoyzia (grasses that are usually cut shorter than rye), backspin may occur on almost every shot with a lofted club.

ALERT!

Don't assume that if you put a backspin on the ball on one course, you can do the same on another. Avoid chasing the stroke you think helped you spin the ball and stick with your basic swing motion. It might have just been the grass.

Surrendering the Impossible Shot

Shot making will help you score better—that is if you've practiced relentlessly and nearly perfected your shots before taking these fancy skills out on the course. Remember that you're supposed to be in control of the ball. If that means you need to employ the same old, boring basic swing motion to remain in control, then do so. By all means, practice shot making, but don't take it out on the course until you've mastered it.

One problem with golfers of all skill levels is the desire to hit a shot they have no business trying to hit. This isn't the shot from behind a tree or out of the rough, but the shot off the tee and into the fairway, or from the fairway into the green. Every golf course will tempt you to hit shots that are impossible, or if not impossible, improbable.

Cutting Dog Legs

Short courses often tempt with dog legs (a section of a hole, usually halfway between the tee and the green, that has a sharp bend). For discussion purposes, imagine a hole that's a short, par four, dog leg to the right. The dog-legged hole is designed to make the golfer leave the driver in the bag and play a shorter first shot in order to have a straight second shot into the green. However, some players attempt to hit the driver over the dog leg to shorten their second shot by a considerable distance, or even to put the tee shot on the green. If you're consistent with your driver and confident of the carry necessary to clear the tall trees and the woods that create the dog leg, go for it if the distance of that tee shot is standard for you. But if it's at the edge of your abilities, ask yourself what could you gain, and what could you possibly lose?

For starters, you might land on the green and two putt for a birdie. Or you might land away from the green, which means a chip, pitch, or short iron, and in all probability a two putt for par. Now look at what you could lose. If the ball doesn't carry, you're in the woods. If the ball slices, you're deeper into the woods. If the ball hooks, given the extra distance the driver provides, you may miss the fairway to the left and find trouble there. All this for a chance to barely improve the odds for a birdie.

FACT

The Vardon Trophy is given to the professional golfer with the lowest average score per round. Usually the Vardon winner finished a given year with an average in the neighborhood of 68.5 shots per round. Since pros are normally on courses rated with pars from 70 to 72, the finest average score of golfers making a living at the game is about three under par per round.

On the other hand, you could play the dog leg the prudent way: Hit a long iron into the fairway, leaving a seven iron into the green. The pin is 158 yards away. Your seven iron carries 150 yards. At worst, with a good shot, you're some twenty feet away after the shot, with a chance for birdie or a certain par. Enough said.

A Green Sloping Toward Water or a Bunker

Say you've got the perfect lie and the perfect distance for a wedge to the pin. It's early in the morning, and the fairway is wet and the greens are hard. If you can hit the ball just behind the pin and spin the ball, you're in line for an easy birdie. So, you go for it.

Moisture acts just like grass between club face and ball. The ball may fly more and/or spin less. What's likely to happen (on wet fairways or dry) is, if the ball hits the slope, the ball probably won't back up with spin. It will probably bounce, then roll into the water or bunker on the backside.

The safe shot would be to take a little off the wedge and put the ball on the front of the green some twenty to thirty feet from the flag. Hitting short would take all the trouble out of play, and you'd still have an opportunity for birdie.

Bogie Is the Beginner's Friend

There's a good chance that no one will tell the beginner that the bogie is a friend, but it is. Think of par for those early rounds of golf as a bogie for each hole, that is, one over par. In other words, if a hole is par four (meaning two shots to get on the green and two putts), think of that hole as par five (three to get on and two putts). This will train you early to take trouble out of play. It will help keep you from trying shots you have no business trying, and from trying too hard to compensate for one bad shot and hitting a second and a third on the same hole.

If you can shoot bogie golf, you'll shoot in the low nineties. Not a bad score for a hacker. Think of all the trouble you'll avoid and all the opportunities that will pop up as pleasant surprises simply by surrendering the impossible shot for the prudent one.

If bogie is your friend, you may decide to lay up (hit a shorter shot) instead of flying over that lake protecting the green's front edge. If bogie is your friend, and you fail to drive the ball far enough on the dog leg to give yourself a straight shot to the green, you'll play a second, shorter straight shot on the diagonal, positioning yourself rather than trying some wild slice to make up for the poorly hit driver. If you can convince yourself as a beginner or as a high handicapper that bogie is your friend, you will make more pars.

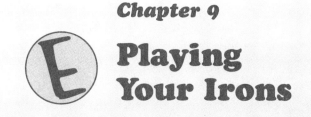

Chapter 9

Playing Your Irons

If you want to improve your game, you need to learn to use your clubs . . . all of your clubs. This chapter will help you to understand the importance of club selection and how to think one shot ahead.

The Difference in the Clubs

From least loft to most loft, clubs in a golf bag range from the putter to the wedges. The clubs work up in increments of three to four degrees of loft from a standard driver with twelve degrees of loft, to a three wood with fifteen degrees, to the wedges. Some golfers have preferences for certain wedges and may carry wedges with as much as sixty degrees of loft (the lob wedge) down to as little as forty-five degrees of loft (a pitching wedge). The higher the loft on a club, the greater the height of the shot—and the greater the possibilities for creating backspin on the ball.

In terms of distance, you hit a golf ball for the least distance with a putter. Putter aside, the greater the loft on a club, the shorter and higher the ball flight. It's also true that higher lofted clubs have shorter shafts than lower lofted clubs. That, too, counts toward the distance a golfer gets from the use of a certain club. The shafts of wedges are shortest. The shafts of the irons get progressively longer as the loft decreases, all the way up to the driver with a shaft of forty-four or forty-five inches depending on the flex of the shaft. Putters are the exception; they don't necessarily fit the rules about length.

Changing Ball Positions for Different Irons

Where a golfer will position a golf ball in reference to the stance mixes art with science, preference with need. How much height does the shot need? Does it need to rise above a tall tree or does the shot need to carry past a distant hazard and roll? Or perhaps it needs to stop quickly after a long carry.

Take Advantage of the Swing's Low Point

By now you're beginning to discover why all the emphasis is on the basic motion of the swing. With the basic swing motion down pat, all you need to do is position the ball so you strike it as the club approaches the low point. The low point of the swing should occur roughly two to three inches inside of the front heel. There will be some slight individual differences, but with enough practice you'll know exactly where your swing's low point occurs. It should occur at the same point regardless of which club you use.

Why doesn't the low point of the swing vary with the length of the shaft?
Because your swing is the same with every club. The length of the club dictates the distance of your feet from the ball.

Ball Position for an Iron off the Tee

The only variation in ball position for a regular iron shot may be when you choose to use an iron off the tee. The operative word is "may." For example, let's say that from all the practice you've had at the range, you know that you hit your three iron 200 yards. When you stand on a par three that is 190 yards to the front of the green with the pin about 15 yards farther on, why would you want to do anything but what you would ordinarily do when hitting that three iron off the ground? The answer is, you wouldn't do anything different . . . except, maybe this: Make sure the ball's lie on the tee box is perfect.

Using a tee (a broken one is usually the perfect choice in this case), press the tee all the way to the ground with the ball, giving it the absolutely perfect lie. Then smack your usual three iron shot, positioned two to three inches inside of your front heel, and watch it land as it usually does about 185 to 190 yards away and roll toward the pin. It will probably roll a bit farther on the green than on the fairway, so the chances are good it will roll all the way to the cup. There are no changes to the ball position, just a confidence boost from a broken tee to make sure the lie is perfect.

In Need of a Change

On the other hand, suppose the par three is 205 yards to the front of the green with another 15 yards to the flag. The tee is elevated, so you believe that you may be able to carry your three iron to the green or at least close, but you aren't sure you can get the ball close to the pin. You could change clubs, but you're afraid that your three wood would send the ball too far, and you don't carry a two iron or a five wood in your golf bag.

Now's the time to tee the ball up and move the ball position forward of the swing's low point, so that the ball is aligned with your front heel. What affect on the ball will this have? Think a moment before you read on. By striking the ball with your three iron at just the beginning of the upswing, you'll impart some topspin on the ball. When the ball hits the ground, it will roll more than it normally would, perhaps all the way to the flag.

FACT

Most teachers of the game no longer adhere to the old rule of "the shorter the iron (and more lofted), the further back the ball is played in the stance." There may be some excellent golfers who still play their irons that way. Most, however, do not.

When More Than One Club Will Do

The best golfers tend to be thinkers. If you've watched more than a couple of tournaments on television, you've probably heard a few players being praised for their creativity with club selection. If you're a beginner, it's probably best not to get creative just yet. You should learn to hit each club as well as you can hit it, master your swing, and find consistency first. Play enough golf, though, and the time will come when you'll know that you need to be creative.

The Major Element in Club Selection

Wind can be a major factor in determining which club you want to hit. Don't worry about those gentle puffs of air that barely penetrate the weave of your clothing. Do concern yourself with those blasts of wind or a steady breeze that cause the flag at the pin to flap madly, or even worse, bend the pin with its force.

Stand on that 200-yard par three again, but this time the wind is directly in your face. The wind is stiff enough that your pant's legs snap against your calves. You could tee up your three iron off your left heel and plan for the roll to compensate for the wind. Or you could make another choice and bring out the three wood, estimating that the breeze is going to knock plenty of yards off the normal flight of the ball.

Making a Choice

Crosswinds can be trickier and demand that you use a club at a distance for which you usually don't consider using it. For instance, if your five iron is usually good for 175 yards and that's the distance you have remaining to the pin, but the crosswind has you worried about holding the target line, then take a lower lofted club and hit "beneath" the wind.

Here's the real choice you face: hit the five iron and make a large adjustment for the crosswind, hoping that it will blow your ball to the target line; or take fate more directly into your owns hands and use a longer club with a lower trajectory, taking more of the wind out of play. In the latter choice, whether the wind gusts or eases, your ball will fly closer to the target line to begin with. The difference is, you'll have to control the distance with an easier swing.

There are times when you can actually hit below the strong currents of the wind, but even when you can't, a ball flying at a lower trajectory off the tee and landing on the ground sooner will be moved less by a crosswind than a high shot will be.

Questions to Ask When Making Club Selection

Here's what to ask yourself as you decide on the right club for your next shot:

- How far must the ball carry?
- How much roll do I need?
- How will the wind alter ball flight?
- Am I better off missing the target line to the left or to the right?
- If the ball doesn't stop where I want it to, am I better off too long or too short?

When More Than One Distance Will Do

It's impressive to watch a golfer pull out a wedge from 100 yards and send the ball soaring high into the air where the ball reaches its zenith, falls, and lands just a few feet from the hole. It's just as impressive to see a golfer hit past the pin and spin the shot back toward the hole. But at the end of a round, the only thing that is impressive is the total on the scorecard.

Pick to Score

If the wind is forcefully blowing or gusting, launching a high wedge shot lowers your chances of getting the ball close to the pin. Given the earlier discussion about wind, that should be obvious. Launching a high shot you usually control into an unpredictable breeze pairs skill with chance. Sometimes there's no other way, but often there is.

Suppose the green you're approaching is guarded by bunkers on three sides: left, right, and rear. The wind is gusting from zero to fifteen miles per hour diagonally into your face from between the bunker on the right and the bunker behind the green.

ALERT!

While you may be tempted to stick with what you know and trust a usual club to send the ball a usual distance, it's always better to first take a look at all options. There are several factors that can affect ball flight. Remember that golf is as much a mind game as a physical game.

Let's say with no wind your wedge shot is always good for 95 to 102 yards, depending on how well you hit it. If the breeze were constant, you could consider backing up a club (to a nine iron) and letting the wind work with your shot to control the distance and direction. But the wind is gusting. You can try to pick a moment to hit your shot when the wind is calm, but just as you strike the ball, the wind could gust again. A gusting wind means that all three bunkers are in play if you use the nine iron. The bunkers on the left and right are in play if your use your wedge.

Your solution may be to play the ball to a different distance and pull out an eight iron from your bag. Because an eight iron has less loft than the nine iron and wedge, the ball will "run" more when it hits the ground. Let's say you know that with a half swing you can punch an eight iron razor-straight about 80 yards. Forget about a 100-yard shot and think 80 yards, with a 10- to 20-yard run after the ball hits the ground. Even if the ball comes up short, you've taken the bunkers out of play and still have an opportunity for a good score on the hole.

Choosing a Location for Your Next Shot

If you play on a hilly course with a lot of slopes, instead of using the driver on the tee or a three iron for a second shot on a long par five, you might choose a shorter club in order to place your ball in a better spot for the next shot. There might be a nice area that will give you a better lie, promising a better shot to the green.

Of course, it's not as impressive as crushing a drive from the tee, but a well-placed three wood used to deter the risk of having to hit from a slope, and to increase the chances of an excellent subsequent shot, has obvious, if less macho, rewards. Shots are much more accurate when you can assume your proper stance and hit with your best swing.

Choosing a Distance for Your Next Shot

You've arrived at the eighteenth hole. Let's say you don't par very often and bogies make you happy, but if you can just par this last hole, you'll break 100 for the first time. Or, you could be a pro, and a par or birdie on the eighteenth could win the tournament. To achieve the respective goals in either situation, you need to put yourself in position so that your next shot (the shot from the fairway) will get you close to the pin. You also know that there are certain distances that you hit certain clubs.

If you were to listen to a pro consult his or her caddie about distances, you wouldn't hear, "It's 'about' 150 yards from here." What you would hear instead is, "It's 147 yards to the front of the green, and 6 yards to the flag"; or, "It's 200 yards to carry that fairway bunker"; or, "That maple tree is 230 yards from here, leaving you a full wedge to the hole." What pro and caddie are trying to decide is how far to hit this shot in order to position the ball for the absolute best, most accurate shot on the next one. They're thinking one shot ahead.

This may mean hitting short on this shot in order to use a full swing on the next. You might also try to hit a certain distance now, so that your next shot can be with the club you're most consistent with.

FACT

The object of every golf shot is not to see how far you can hit the ball, how high you can make it go, or how much you can spin it. The object of every golf shot is to hit the best, most effective shot you can hit. Sometimes the best shot is a shorter shot.

Short Shots

Short shots are shots from 100 yards and in. In the modern game, short shots are both art and science, feel and mechanics. Short shots have developed in importance over the past forty years as developments in fairway grasses have allowed for more fairways to be cut tight (shorter). Short shots have always been important, certainly, but whereas once many shots from many fairways across the country included blades of grass between the ball and the club face, today that's rarely the case. Grass between ball and club face made the shots more unpredictable as to trajectory and spin. With shorter fairways making trajectory and spin more discernible these days, there are fewer excuses on short shots for not getting the ball close.

Short-Shot Panic

Some golfers have difficulty learning to control short shots. Some tend to raise up while swinging the club on short shots. They'll undo their torso tilt and often unbend at the knees while trying to finesse a short shot close to the flag. For others, their brain will override what they know about good swing motion. When the time comes to deploy a less lengthy shot, their body seems to forget the lessons it has learned. Even though you know that hitting down on the ball gives it its height, your brain wants to tell your body that to get the ball up into the air for shots within 100 yards, you must try to lift the ball, to scoop it.

Slowing the Swing

Slowing their swing is the second reason golfers have difficulty with short shots. One golfer might not notice this problem when watching another try to lift the ball, but an experienced player will notice it. (It even happens on the pro circuit from time to time.) A golfer will decelerate the club head as it approaches impact with the ball to soften, or shorten, the shot. That's just another example of brain overriding a good lesson about the golf swing. Decelerating the swing has no positive effect on the shot, it only makes the shot less controllable.

When You Need a Shorter Swing

The only cure for trying to lift the ball is to practice until your body either overrides your brain, or your brain trusts your swing motion. The cure for a decelerating swing is a shorter swing. When do you need to have a shorter swing? Certainly when you're standing under the low limb of a tree, but more often, you need it for the shorter shots.

Don't panic. You know what to do to get a golf ball to fly into the air: Use the basic swing motion and allow the club to hit down on the ball just before the low point of the swing.

Shorter Swings Control Club-Head Acceleration

The science of a shorter shot is in the shortened backswing. The shorter the backswing, the less the club-head acceleration. The club head has less time and distance over which to accelerate. Otherwise the swing motion is the same. Remember you're trying to keep the basic swing motion for absolutely every shot you possibly can. Keeping the same basic swing motion generates consistency and better scoring.

The art of the shorter shot is in how much the golfer needs to shorten the backswing for a given distance with a certain club. Sorry, but there's no series of easy-to-follow steps to guarantee consistent distance in a shorter shot. There's just a one-step plan: practice.

Make the backswing fit with how much you want the club head to accelerate on the downswing. Distance is determined by the amount of club-head acceleration, not the amount of deceleration.

FACT

High handicappers often try to lift the ball on short shots rather than let the club come down through the ball. As a result they skull a lot of shots; that is, they hit the ball with the blade and send it scurrying much farther than desired. Fear of skulling the ball leads to deceleration, and even poorer shots that scoot wide to the right and left.

Wrist Action

Many beginning golfers believe that extra wrist action is a necessary ingredient for shots inside of 100 yards. But it's the shorter backswing that makes the ball fly higher, shorter, and with more spin. Learn to use your backswing properly to control the flight of the ball on short shots.

ALERT!

Extra wrist action requires more practice than beginners are likely to have gotten, and more practice than high handicappers are usually willing to apply to their games.

However, there may be times when more wrist is called for. Let's say you're close to the green but separated from the pin by a bunker and a small amount of green. When properly applied, extra wrist action can help get the ball into the air quicker and higher and with plenty of backspin to help it stop more quickly. Here's how it works: Cock the wrists when pulling the club back on a reduced backswing and add to the club-head acceleration on the downswing by uncocking the wrists. (E)

Chapter 10

Chipping and Pitching

Chipping and pitching are critical to scoring well. A chip shot is a short approach shot struck with a lofted club that carries the ball a desired distance (usually short) and runs toward the pin. A pitch is a lofted approach shot that carries further and rolls less. Learning these skills early can help any golfer have more fun.

A Whole New Set of Rules

You won't be using the basic swing motion for these shots, but it will serve as a point of reference for chipping and pitching. Chipping and pitching are about distance control—controlling the distance of both carry and roll. Off of the tee, a carry that's shorter or longer than planned, followed by a roll that's less than what a golfer had hoped for, probably won't make a great deal of difference in the final score on that hole. However, a difference of even a few feet in carry or roll of a pitch can easily amount to an extra stroke or more.

A golfer can have a great game from tee to within fifty yards of the green and still lack an ability to score well. Likewise, a golfer can have mediocre swing mechanics, yet possess a good touch around the green and keep his or her score competitive.

A New Rule for Carry and Distance

A pitch shot comes in two varieties: the pitch and the pitch and run. A pitch carries farther and rolls less; a pitch and run carries shorter and rolls more. Both shots can be used from an identical distance over the same ground to achieve the same purpose. The difference is in the design of the shot. Here's a good rule of thumb: A pitch should carry two-thirds of the distance to the hole and roll one-third; the pitch and run carries only one-third of the distance and rolls two-thirds of the way to the hole.

 FIGURE 10-1

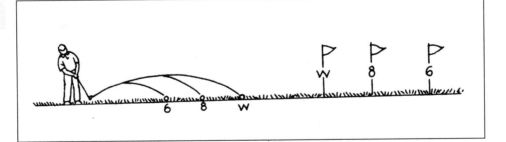

▲ Pitching with the wedge produces two-thirds carry, one-third run. Pitching with a six iron produces one-third carry, two-thirds run.

FACT

Chipping and pitching mean different things to different people. To some they are synonymous. In this chapter, a "chip" is an approach shot with short carry and a longer run, and a "pitch" is an approach shot with a longer carry and very short run. "Pitch and run" is a shot with short carry and a longer run and will be used synonymously with "chip."

A New Rule for Club Usage

Suppose you're standing on the tee. If you need a ball to carry 220 yards and then roll as far as it can, you'll use your driver because no other club could do the job. When it comes to pitches and chips, at ten yards off the green with sixty feet of green in front of the hole, any number of clubs in your bag could meet the requirement: your putter or a three wood, at the extreme; a five iron; a seven or eight iron; or even a wedge.

Part of the decision is feel, part has to do with terrain, part may have to do with slope. For instance, if the ten yards between your ball and the green contains a bunker, you won't be using your putter or your three wood. You'll need a lofted club to be sure you carry the bunker.

The Right Clubs to Use

Some instructors argue that only certain clubs can be used from near the green, but a viewing of a pro tournament will demonstrate that pros, given the same shot near the green, will choose a variety of clubs to get the same result. In fact, listen carefully to the commentator, and you'll often hear that "so-and-so" landed in this same spot yesterday, but yesterday he used club x, while today he's using club y.

The right clubs to use will vary with the individual, according to experience, touch, and sometimes intuition. It will take some practice to find out. Generally, however, the higher your handicap or the newer you are to the game, the less loft you'll want on the club. If you're hoping for early success around the greens, you'll want to put the ball on the ground earlier and let it roll more.

The best thing for the beginner to remember is not which club, but what distances—the one-third carry, two-thirds run rule for a pitch and run; and the two-thirds carry, one-third run rule for the pitch shot. Most beginners will find success quicker by sticking with the pitch and run wherever possible.

Weight Shift

With pitching and chipping, most of the weight shifting you do comes with the setup. You won't begin with the weight centered, and the weight won't shift around the fixed axis toward the inside of your back leg and through the swing to the finish on the inside of your front leg. For this part of your game, you'll want a "quiet" lower body. Pitching and chipping aren't about power, but about touch and feel.

Eliminating Power to Increase Feel

If you've ever watched college or professional basketball, you may have noticed that the big guys, the centers, seem to have the most difficult time making free throws. This doesn't have anything to do with lack of practice. One reason for their difficulty has to do with power. Bigger players are more powerful and closer to the basket because of height and longer arms. The bigger more powerful player has to work to eliminate power from the shot.

All basketball players reduce leg power to make free throws. Most have a much simpler hand motion, a motion that delivers all the power necessary for these uncontested shots. The big guys, already closer to the basket by height and arm span and more powerful because of body mass, have to take even more out of the motion of their free throws to reduce power and increase control on the shot.

For pitching the golf ball, the most effective way to take power out of the equation is to keep the lower body quiet. You simply don't need leg drive to launch these shots.

Shift Weight Forward on Setup

Shifting the weight onto the front foot at the setup is the best way to keep your legs out of the shot. Place your feet parallel to the target line and pretend you're setting up a normal shot. Start with your weight balanced as you've learned to do. Now shift the weight forward so that about 70 percent of your body weight is over your front leg. This is the proper location for your weight when you set up for a pitch shot. It's the proper location for your weight, but not for your feet.

Open Your Stance

Instead of placing your feet parallel to the target line, pull your front foot back from the line. Open your stance a bit, so that the front of your body begins to face the target. Be sure to adjust your feet so that the stance, open with weight shifted, is comfortable.

FACT

For most golfers, a comfortable stance means that the toes on both feet turn slightly toward the target. This open stance helps take the hips out of the shot, too.

Stiff Wrists

Think back to the basic swing motion for a moment. The legs and hips, the most powerful parts of your body, begin the swing. The torso, with its back, chest, and shoulder muscles, continue the generation of power. The torso frees the arms, the weakest and quickest body parts where the swing is concerned, to do what they do best: provide the whipping action to manufacture top speed for the club head. For pitch shots, you want to take the speed of the club head out of the equation, but not club-head acceleration. Your aim is to reduce your capacity for club-head speed. and your stance and stiff wrists will help to do this.

Put your wristwatch on the wrist closest to the target at setup. When you use the basic swing motion you've learned, the club face will rotate throughout the swing, as will your wrist. But, when pitching the golf ball, your wristwatch will face the target from setup, through backswing, through finish. This fuses your wrists with your arms. Maintaining these stiff wrists means that the only speed the club head can now generate will be supplied by the turn of the torso.

QUESTION?

Why slow the chip with stiff wrists, rather than just slowing down the motion?
Thrust management. Cocking the wrists adds power to the swing. The aim of chipping is to eliminate power and create better distance control. There's also no angular momentum in the chipping motion.

The Constant Club Face

If you've just taken a few swings while keeping your wristwatch toward the target line, you may have noticed another equally important function of the stiff wrist. The club face, staying in line with the front wrist, never moves either. You've not only reduced the speed the wrists help to generate, but the club face never changes in relation to the target. It will stay square to the target line. There are some players who employ more wrist action, and do it quite successfully. However, for most players, keeping the wrist stiff and the club face square to the target line will help to hit the ball accurately, putting it where they want it to go.

It may help you to make consistent pitch shots if you think of the pitch as an exaggerated putt. The club stays on line with the target, never (or barely) leaving that line through the backswing. Whereas a putting stroke may have a maximum backswing of only about a foot, the pitch, depending on distance needed, may extend up as high as the waist.

The action of the club is similar to the action a golfer will use with a putter. The square face of the club used for pitching the ball will stay on the target line. The club will be brought back on the target line, just like a putter is brought back on that path. Where the action differs is that the club will swing on more of an arc from down at address, to up perhaps as high as the waist, then back down, and with a follow-through that may end as high as the waist. If you look at a pitch from behind, the club face will appear to raise, lower, and raise up and down and up a nearly perpendicular line from the ball to the sky and back to the ball.

Hitting Down for Height

This is probably striking a chord in your memory. There are some things about golf that bear repeating over and over. Doing some things consistently from the get-go helps even the greenest golfing rookie start out enjoying the game. Hit down for height. Hit down for height. Never, never try to sweep the ball on a pitch or to lift it with the club. The hands, even on the pitch, are aligned at address in the same position as on the basic swing. This position helps to keep the low point of the swing beneath or in front of the ball, assuring that you'll strike the ball with a downward motion and get it up into the air.

FACT

You can flog the ball down the fairway and brutalize another shot, missing the green by a wide margin, but if you can pitch the ball close and knock it in, you'll save a lot of shots. Shots become more important the closer you get to the hole.

Begin your mastery of pitches by placing the ball in the ball's usual position two to three inches inside your left heel. Learn to strike this shot consistently. Once you have confidence with the shot, you can learn to customize the pitch when the grass of the rough requires an even steeper club angle to prevent grass from grabbing the club, or when the shot needs a little more height and a little less roll.

Adjust Ball Position Further Back in Your Stance

Instead of positioning the golf ball two to three inches inside your left heel, try positioning it four to five inches away from the left heel and more toward the right. The further back in your stance, the greater the angle of the downswing striking the ball.

Adjust Ball Position Closer to Your Stance

With the basic swing motion, you've learned to let the shaft of the club dictate your distance from the ball. That means the shaft of the driver keeps your feet farther from the ball, and the shaft of a wedge brings them closest. It also means that swing path is shallower on a driver and steeper on a wedge. By moving a few inches closer to the ball, so that your toes are only eight to ten inches away, you can steepen the angle of the swing even more to help reduce the dangers of pitching from the rough, and to get more loft on the shot.

Warnings

Practically everything you've learned about pitching the golf ball has assumed a good lie on the fairway. Learn to pitch and to pitch and run the ball from this perfect surface first. Develop confidence in your ability to get the ball close to the pin from a good lie just off the green. The truth is, the more you play, the more you'll be pitching the ball from good lies as your accuracy improves. But good player or bad, pro or beginner, when the ball is resting on a surface other than a fairway, there are no guarantees about ball flight.

The number one cause of topping a pitch shot (striking the ball above it's center) is allowing your elbows to pull apart, changing the shape of your swing. Address the ball. The distance between your elbows should remain nearly constant throughout the entire pitch.

Pitching from the Greenside Rough

The taller grass of the rough means two bad things: unpredictable spin and height on a pitch shot, and uncertainty about ball strike.

Anytime grass stands between the ball and the club, the grass will affect the ball strike. Sometimes the ball comes out of the rough behaving as though struck cleanly. More often, it flies out faster and lands harder (rolls farther).

You have to make decisions about how you're going to strike this ball from the rough near the green. Regardless of your decision—to hit it normally or to hit it more softly—you're apt to be wrong as often as you're right. In fact, if it were possible to hit the same ball from the identical situation a dozen times, the ball probably wouldn't behave the same way twice. So, make your decision, have confidence in it, strike the ball, and take your medicine.

That medicine may include the ball scooting hard to the right either with loft (lucky you) or zipping across the green and off (way off!) faster than a scared rabbit. Grass has a tendency to grab the toe of the club, opening the club face and sending the ball way off target. If the grass grabs the toe and stops the club on its downward path, the blade may strike the ball rather than the club face, sending the ball bulletlike to someplace you never wanted it to go.

Learn to use a wide-open club face. Experiment with your wedge. Start with the club face square to the target. Then lay the club face back, giving it even more loft. To hit the ball toward your target, open your stance and aim left of the target. An open club face helps the club slip through rough more efficiently.

Pitching from a Bermuda Fringe

There the ball sits, on top of the wiry, warm-climate grass as though it were teed up. It looks rather innocent just off the green. The grass may not even be that tall, two, maybe three, inches. You don't think that you'll have any trouble getting this ball into the air. You employ your stroke for pitching the ball with a wedge. You keep the club face square, you hit down, and the ball flies up four or five inches and flops back down, barely in front of where it was before your stroke. Maybe it flies up just about the way you planned the shot, but instead of landing ten yards away and rolling to the flag, it lands three yards away and stops twenty-five feet from the pin.

On the flip side, if the ball is nestled down in the Bermuda at greenside, you had better start pulling out the lucky charms. If your ball is snuggled down in the Bermuda a long distance from the green, you'd probably pull out a wedge, plan a steep swing, and strike the ball with everything you've got, hoping to get it close. At the edge of the green, a full swing might be just the ticket to get the ball up and to the pin, or it might send the ball clear into the next county. A pitch might lift the ball beautifully or hardly move it at all. Plan your shot, and hit confidently, knowing that there are no sure things in this situation.

Pitching from Hard Ground

Since you've mastered the basic swing motion, you know that hitting the ball with a full swing off hard ground can make for a great shot. The club will hit down on the ball, pinching it and sending it toward the green with plenty of backspin to hold the ball once it lands near the flag. Why shouldn't this pitch shot be just as effective?

Your weight never shifts on a chip. It starts left and stays left. It's left at setup, stays left on the backswing, left at impact, and left on the finish. More or less, 70 percent of your weight should be on your left foot throughout the pitch.

The truth is you might hit it perfectly from this lie. But with a pitch shot, you won't generate club-head speed, which also means you won't generate greater mass in the club head (remember your high school physics?). If you strike a mere trace behind the ball on a pitch from hard ground, the sole of the club likely will bounce, sending a blistering worm burner across the green and into more trouble.

To ensure a downward stroke, be mindful of hand position—keep your hands in front of the ball. Consider increasing the steep angle of your swing a bit by moving slightly closer to the ball, and/or by positioning the ball a small distance further back in your stance. Ⓔ

Chapter 11

Playing from Bunkers

Bunkers are the beginner's or high handicapper's nightmare. However, depending on the lie and the location, a shot from bunkers may not be much harder to make than a shot from the fairway. It's just a matter of knowing what you're up against and learning to play with skill.

Different Types of Bunkers

When you think of bunkers, you usually think sand. At least, golfers in America do. The are some grass bunkers here and there, but an avid American golfer could play golf his or her entire life and never have to hit out of a grass bunker or a pothole bunker. But if you were to play in Scotland or the rest of Europe, you'll find grass bunkers and potholes.

Grass bunkers resemble most American sand traps, only they have tall grass in the bottom, not sand. Potholes are deep holes and not very large, usually requiring a ball to be hit almost straight up to get it free. This chapter will focus on sand traps, since that's what you will most likely encounter. However, it is a good idea to at least be familiar with the other types of bunkers.

The Problem with the Soft Lie

The sand is not soft in all traps. Sometimes it depends on the type of sand. Often it depends on conditions of rain, the course watering schedule, or whether the traps have recently been turned and the sand loosened.

The Soft Problem

Soft sand presents challenges different from those of a hard surface. For instance, in sand, spin can't be generated on a ball when the golfer uses a normal swing. Care has to be taken in club selection and in swing control so that the club doesn't dig into the sand, barely moving the ball. In soft sand, a golfer wants the club to "bounce" off the sand so that it will not dig in.

Make the Swing Shallow

To help assure that the club will bounce and reduce the chances of it digging in, you must change the angle of your swing to a shallower swing. As a point of reference, the basic swing motion helps the golfer achieve a swing path of about forty-five degrees. A swing path much above forty-five degrees—swinging more upright—is steep, and less than forty-five degrees is shallow. You'll need to bring the club back lower, rather than higher. This will help prevent you from beating down on the ball and burying the club.

Bring It On

Before we go much further in discussing how to escape the dreaded sand trap, let's first discuss your attitude. Many beginners are terrified of bunkers, so much so that they spend more of their time worrying about landing in the bunker than concentrating on proper swing path and aim. As you know, when special attention is given to trouble, trouble often finds itself coming into play.

FACT

The rules of golf do not permit you to "ground" the club in the sand. In other words, you can't place the head of the club on the ground to help you line up for the shot. Grounding the club is a one-stroke penalty.

While you certainly don't want to aim for the sand, try not to be so worried about your ball landing there. Hitting from the sand is not an impossible shot. In fact, hitting from hard sand with a good lie isn't much more difficult than hitting from the fairway. One of the main differences is in the golfer's attitude toward the attempt.

If you fear the sand, the sand will get the best of you. If you keep your fear in check and concentrate instead on making the right club selection, maintaining balance and control, determining the best shot, and following the suggestions in this chapter, you'll likely escape the sand not much worse for the wear.

If you simply can't erase that fear from your mind, then get out there and practice alone without the pressure of others watching you. The more comfortable you become in the sand, the less you'll fear it and the better shots you'll make.

Fairway Bunker Shots and an Embedded Ball

The best advice any golfer can receive regarding an embedded (partially buried) ball in a fairway bunker is take your punishment and move on. That means you should pick the safest, easiest way out of the bunker (the way least likely to get you into more trouble and most likely to get you out of it) and hit it.

Fortunately, most balls landing in fairway bunkers don't land on the fly; they enter on the roll. When a ball enters on a roll, you'll probably get a good lie with the ball sitting on top of flat sand. The ball won't be all too difficult to hit from this position. However, if the ball comes from the sky and lands in the sand, it will likely embed itself in a small crater. Getting the club head to hit the ball correctly in this position is a lot more difficult.

Don't Be a Hero

More strokes are lost by golfers of all abilities trying to salvage a bad situation than are lost by golfers who accept the fact that the best way out of the bunker won't advance the ball to the green. By taking a realistic approach, you'll most likely clear the ball from the bunker in one direction or other by a few yards. Even though this may seem as though you aren't getting anywhere, you're getting out of the bunker—isn't that what's important at the moment?

Beat the Ball

So how do you get out of the bunker? Take a high-lofted club and adjust your stance so that the ball is played further back—further toward your back foot to steepen the angle at which the ball will be struck on the down stroke. That's almost too gentle a description. Beat down on that ball as though it's threatening your life. Practice will tell you how much farther back to place that ball and which clubs you can make work best for you.

Work your feet into the sand to secure your position. Most golfers open the face of the club to help the club slip or knife through the sand. They open their stance so that their bodies and swing paths aim slightly in the opposite direction from the open club face. (For a right-handed golfer, the club face will aim to the right of the target line and the stance will aim to the left.) Then take a swing, knowing that your full swing will likely move the ball a matter of ten yards or so. Be sure you follow through with the swing.

ALERT!

Always rake away the evidence of your presence in the bunker. Smooth over the sand blasted by your shot, and rake away all footprints.

Fairway Bunker Shots and a Good Lie

Most of the time, balls landing in fairway bunkers won't embed. That doesn't mean your lie will be a "good" lie. The ball may roll too close to the lip of the bunker, in which case you should just take your medicine. On the other hand, many times the ball will roll to a stop near the center of the trap making escape reasonably simple and keeping the green an achievable target.

Hitting off a Hard Sand Lie

If the sand in the fairway bunker is compacted, you have the best possible opportunity for your next shot. Simply take the club you would normally hit from that distance away from the green and take your normal shot. The ball should carry somewhat normally off that lie.

Hitting off a Soft Sand Lie

The ball won't fly as far off of a soft lie as it will off of a harder lie. Some golfers insist that's because a hard lie actually helps the ball travel further; the pinching action helps with ball compression off the face of the club. It could also be that no matter how cleanly you strike the ball, you'll also take some sand with the shot, and sand will reduce the flight of the ball.

The most effective rule for hitting a ball that is sitting on top of soft sand in the fairway trap is to take one club more than you would ordinarily hit from that spot if you were on the fairway. For example, if you have 150 yards to the green, and for you that's usually a five iron, use a four iron instead. You'll probably get the same results. Experience will help you for this situation. For some golfers it will take two clubs more to achieve the same distance off of soft sand. In which case (using the same example), exchange the usual five iron for a three iron instead.

While playing from the bunkers is probably not a part of your golf game you want to repeat over and over, it's still a good idea to practice shots from the bunkers whenever you get a chance. With more practice, you'll build confidence that will take the edge off of having to make a shot from the sand, thus increasing your chances for a good escape.

Greenside Bunkers and the Lie

Your play from a greenside bunker (one that's right next to the putting green) is dictated by the lie that you have. On a typical greenside bunker with a good lie and the ball resting atop the sand, the setup will be the same as with a pitch and run shot. Open your stance. Put your weight forward (70 percent onto the front foot), with your shoulders and hips a little open—aimed a little left of the target. Using a sand wedge or a lob wedge, you hit the shot, letting the sand carry the ball up and onto the green.

How to Hit the Ball

Some teachers, as a means of illustrating the type of shot needed to get the ball up and out to the green, place a dollar bill below an inch of sand and set a golf ball on top. "Hit the front edge of the bill," they'll say, "and lift the dollar out." The idea is pretty good, actually. The general rule is that you should strike the sand about two inches behind the ball, with the low point of the swing coming at its usual point at or just in front of the ball.

FIGURE 11-1

◀ When you assume your stance, work your feet into the sand to stabilize yourself, and don't ground the club.

A Soft, Fluffy Lie Changes the Shot

In any realm there's no substitute for experience. Play enough sand shots and you'll learn that the softer the sand, the closer to your ball you'll want your wedge to hit. Just how close is difficult to say. That decision is partly a matter of instinct and experience, as well as the particular characteristics of your own swing. If you've developed a consistent swing and plan to practice sand shots from softer lies, aim to strike the sand about an inch behind the ball instead of two, and make your soft, fluffy lie adjustments from there.

Ball Carry Requirements Change the Shot

The further behind the ball you hit, the shorter the carry, regardless of the lie. So, carrying the ball ten yards or twenty yards will be determined more by the distance behind the ball the blade strikes, and not the speed of the swing. A lot of greenside bunker play on most courses set up for amateurs requires no more than the swing you would use for a pitch and run.

Hitting out of a Footprint

It shouldn't happen but it does, some golfer on the course ahead of you forgot to cleanup after him- or herself. Your ball lands in a footprint and you're left with a much more difficult shot. The ball will probably fly out of the sand with overspend and roll farther.

You could try the heroic shot and attempt to pick the ball clean from the sand (a very, very difficult shot), but you're likely to either leave the ball almost where it lies or blade the ball, which could bury it or send it rocketing across the green. Or, you could take your medicine and strike the sand behind the ball, making certain the ball gets out of the bunker. It may roll too far, but the trouble you'll get into from taking your medicine is likely to be not nearly so bad as trying the low-percentage shot.

QUESTION?

What does "blade the ball" mean?
The upper part of the ball is struck by the edge of the club face, causing the ball to hug the ground in flight.

Greenside Bunker Shots to Elevated Greens

One of the challenges elevated greens present is that they reduce the effective use of backspin. The closer to the green you are, the more that's true. Spin is much more effective the higher you can get a shot that will land on the green.

A greenside bunker beside an elevated green compounds the problem. Since you're hitting from up close, it's already difficult to loft the ball enough to use the spin you may be able to put on it. And since the shot is from the bunker, your ability to produce spin on the shot is already significantly reduced.

Open the club face. Lay it wide open. Aim well to the left of the target, because the open club face will send the ball to the right. Then take your stroke. The open club face will increase loft and help you hit a softer shot.

Balance is very important at all times, and especially when playing from the sand. Because the sand doesn't offer much traction, you should bury your feet somewhat to add stability, and open your stance a bit to maintain better balance, and in turn, better control.

Greenside Bunker Shots with a Close Pin

If you're just beginning to play, you may not have noticed how close to greenside bunkers the pin is usually set for the tournament's final day. In fact, you may not know that from day to day on your own course the position of the pin will differ. For the local course repositioning the pin serves two purposes: It helps keep the green from wearing out in certain places, and it gives a different look to the hole, calling for different judgments each time that hole is played. Sometimes at the local course, the pin will be set close to a greenside bunker. Many times on the pro tour, pin placements will be tucked next to bunkers to make the hole tougher to play.

Every decade or so, you're likely to witness a pro tournament in which a ball in the trap has landed in a footprint. Unfortunately for amateurs, it can happen way too often—someone forgets to rake out the bunker as he or she leaves. Sorry, but you've got to hit it as it lies.

The Intimidating Pin

A pin close to a bunker discourages the golfer from hitting an approach shot at the pin. Why? Because a ball in a bunker close to the pin, with only three to six yards of green to work with, makes getting up and down very hard. Golf balls fly out of bunkers with less predictable spin and with less predictable distance control. When a golfer has thirty feet of green to work with, chances are good the ball will land between the golfer and the pin and roll some distance toward the hole. With only nine to eighteen feet, the chances are better than good that the ball will land near or past the hole and run on farther away.

Master the Two-Inch Rule First

The more sand you take on your sand shot, the shorter the distance the ball will carry. The less sand you take on your shot, the more the ball carries. Learn to judge the distances you need by first mastering the sand shot where the club meets the sand two inches behind the ball. Learn how far the ball carries. Get that one shot consistent. Hitting two inches behind the ball on a sand shot will get you out of more trouble than anything else you can do. Once that shot is consistent, and only after it is consistent, try hitting one inch behind the ball, and then three inches behind, learning when not to vary the standard shot.

ALERT!

Always use the two-inch standard as your point of reference. Until it's consistent, forget about shortening or lengthening your sand shot by digging into various amounts of sand. This sand shot standard will save the beginner and the high handicapper more strokes from the bunkers than anything else you can do.

Become a Sand Artist

Da Vinci didn't do Mona Lisa by numbers, and you cannot learn to dance like Fred Astaire at an Arthur Murray Studio. Watch a tournament and you will see pros do things from the sand you aren't going to learn in this book, or any other. You'll see full swings from the sand with the pin so close they can almost hold their wedge out and touch it.

That is not the shot for you. It's not the shot for a midhandicapper, and it may not be the shot for a scratch golfer, either. It's an artist's shot. If you have the talent, and if you have the desire and the time to put in hours of practice over many days and months, then you, too, can be an artist from the sand. Until then, follow your rules, and admire those who can break them so exquisitely.

Chapter 12
Putting

Once you reach the green, you're faced with a new set of challenges. To make a great putt requires several things from you: reading the green, making judgment calls, controlling the speed and distance of the ball, and aiming accurately. This chapter offers tips and suggestions to help you face these challenges and sink that putt.

Great Putting Makes a Great Round

Talk to fine golfers after a round of golf and many will link their score on a round to how well they putted. Think of it like this: Par for a given hole is determined by the number of shots it's supposed to take you to reach the green, plus two puts. A golfer who says he or she scored well usually means that the golfer took fewer putts than he or she might usually take. On eighteen holes, thirty-six putts to a round means the golfer averaged two putts per hole. On a hole where the golfer hit an approach to within two feet, he or she probably one-putted, from sixty feet the golfer may have three-putted.

FACT

The pros who are known on the tour as the best putters are usually those who built their reputations during the time they put their approach shots closer to the pin more often than their competitors. Shorter putts make for great stats.

There's another side to great putting that may have very little to do with developing excellent touch or reading the greens well. It's called luck. On some rounds, good golf shots wind up being great golf shots, and golfers get to take more than their fair share of short putts and fewer than their fair number of thirty footers. Still, there are plenty of things every golfer can do, beginner to pro, to reduce the number of putts required from any distance away from the hole.

Controlling Speed

Controlling the speed of a putt is the only absolute the golfer has in his or her arsenal. At the most basic level, you have to hit an uphill putt harder than a downhill putt—but you still have to control its speed. You may hear a golf commentator say of a pro who just missed a putt to the low side of a hole on a side slope, "right line, not enough speed." Or, when the same putt is missed to the high side, and the pro started the putt on the correct line to the hole, a commentator will often say, "He hit right through the break [the contour of the green]," meaning the putt was hit too fast.

Depending on the speed of the green, and the particular undulations near the hole, a good putter may play more break—count on the ball to curve more and use less speed. On a different green with different undulations, the same good putter may decide to play less break—plan the putt to curve less and hit the putt faster.

Controlling Direction

A good golfer has almost as much control over the direction a putt will take as he or she has over a putt's speed. Assuming the golfer has a consistent stroke and can send the ball off every time on its predetermined course, that putt will usually roll exactly as it was designed to roll. It may miss the hole by an inch or a foot, but if the putt is struck perfectly and if the ball rolls absolutely true, then the putt truly reflects that golfer's best judgment on that shot.

The problem is that greens don't always roll true. There may be ball marks left unrepaired, usually because the indention was so slight it wasn't seen. Golf spikes leave scuff marks. Perhaps the last foursome on the green walked over a certain area of that green repeatedly, leaving a valley of microscopic depth, deep enough only to coax your ball a minute amount in the wrong direction. Your eyes will never catch every blemish that could cause your ball to err, but you can learn to make better judgments and reduce the number of putts you usually require.

There's nothing very good about thirty-six putts in a round of golf. Great golfers would consider a round of twenty-one to twenty-four putts excellent. A round with thirty putts is considered to be about average. A round with thirty-four or more putts is abysmal.

Reading the Green

Good putters read greens well. Add that less-than-exact ability to your skill at controlling the speed and direction of your putt, and you'll hit fewer putts over each round.

Which Way Will Water Flow?

Of course, you shouldn't do this, but if you could dump a bucket of water on a green and watch its direction of flow, you'd notice that the water probably flows in two or three directions as it makes its way downhill. Certainly the slope of a green has a primary direction, but it usually has a few, less obvious, secondary downhill directions, too. Every wiggle in the path of water you poured out is a change of direction that will affect the direction of a putt. If you can see those changes and pick out the different elevations and angles on that slope, you'll become a decent putter as you gain experience.

Overpower Subtle Wavers

It isn't long before every beginning golfer hears some other golfer say about a putt, "Never up, never in." This means that if you don't hit the putt all the way up to the cup, the ball has no chance of finding the bottom of the hole.

Golfers argue over the soundness of that old saying. A putt that died at the hole (lost the last bit of the speed as it approached the hole) might have caught some unseen variation in the green's surface that made the ball change direction dramatically over the last few inches of its roll. The ball might have had enough speed at the beginning to make it all the way toward the cup's center, but something, a blade of grass or a scuff, deflected it.

Watch good golfers stand over those two to three footers. They'll make sure the ball has plenty of speed to go past the hole. They simply aim for the center of the cup and strike the ball with enough force to overcome the weak obstacles that could nudge the putt offline at a slower speed.

The other side of this equation is, of course, what happens if you miss a putt with a fast-rolling ball. Size up the trouble you could get into and make a judgment call. If a ball rolling past a hole and off the green is a worse consequence than a slow ball altering its path by an unseen blemish, good judgment may dictate less speed on the putt.

The Cut of the Green

If you play a round of golf at the end of the day, you may not notice the cut of the green. But if you play early in the morning, you'll plainly see the swaths cut parallel and in opposite directions. The grass on one swath will lie in one direction; the grass on the next swath will lie in the opposite direction. Grass bent toward you slows the ball. Grass bent away from you allows the ball to carry its speed longer.

Speaking of grasses being bent, some greens use "bent grass," a type of grass that, despite its short haircut, bends toward the sun. Even if a green were perfectly flat, a ball will tend to curve in the direction the bent grass is bent. Also, the same rules about ball speed and the direction of other grasses apply to bent grass.

Developing a Pre-Putt Routine

A putt is like any other shot in golf, at least in terms of planning for the shot. Some golfers make a complete circle around the green starting from some distance behind their ball and walking a wide arc to get the feel of undulations, firmness, or sponginess of the surface. They'll stop directly opposite the ball on the far side of the hole, drop down, and restudy the putt. Then they'll get a feel under their feet for the rest of the green along the circle. Other golfers do most of their studying from directly behind their ball and find that that's enough.

Make Your Routine Automatic

A beginner thinks about every step of the routine for each tee shot, each approach, and each putt. With enough playing, the routine before the shot or putt will become so automatic, you won't even think about it. Remember, your brain is like a computer: the data you enter is the data it will spit out. If you approach a putt with doubts, the putt you hit will reflect your worries. Develop a routine that gives you confidence:

* Study the slope of the green.
* Read the grain of the grass.
* Envision the (curved) line your putt must travel.
* Determine the distance you want the ball to travel.

- Determine the direction the putt must go to drop to the hole.
- Decide on speed.

Many of these ingredients of a pre-putt routine are a matter of feel. You'll develop this feel with lots of practice.

After the Calculations

Once you've read the putt in a way that gives you confidence in the decision you made, it's time to line up the putt. You're going to line up the putt in a way similar to the way you line up a shot off the tee, or an approach to the green. Pick a target. (Your target is not the hole, unless the putt is just a few feet, or the green between your ball and the hole is very flat, making the putt dead straight.) Pick out an intermediate target a foot to a few feet in front of your ball, close enough so that the target is along a line on which you plan to start the ball.

Now, line up the head of the putter behind the ball and square to the target line. Sound familiar? Then, set your back foot in position, and now your front foot. Sneak a peak at your intermediate target and putt.

Practice Strokes

Most golfers find a couple of practice strokes helpful in drawing the mind and the stroke in sync. A practice stroke can build the confidence you need to send the putt where you want it to go at the speed you're confident it should be rolling. If you do take a practice stroke, be sure to realign your putter head and readjust your stance afterward.

Aiming the Ball

Many good golfers align the wording on their golf balls with the target line. After determining the direction to start the putt, they crouch behind the ball marker. As they reset the golf ball, and before picking up the ball marker, they align the name of the ball with the target line. Those golfers who include this procedure as part of their pre-putt routine find that it helps them keep their putter in line with the shot.

Other golfers find aligning the ball with the lettering a distraction. If they were to line up the lettering, they would continue to wonder as they hover over the ball if the lettering is properly aimed. Do what gives you confidence. If an element of your routine generates doubts rather than eliminates them, toss it from your routine.

ALERT!

Seize the advantage you have when your ball lies closer to the hole than an opponent's, especially when that other ball is on a line to the hole similar to yours. Go through a pre-putt routine determining speed and slope, and envision the speed and line your putt will take. Then watch the other putt. Use that putt to confirm your read or make minor corrections to it.

Finding Your Best Putting Stroke

The best putting stroke is *your* best putting stroke. Put the 100 best golfers in the world over the same putt and there will be no correlation between putting strokes or styles and the number of putts made. Every good golfer will develop his or her own putting stroke, a stroke that can be repeated easily, a stroke that gives the golfer confidence.

One Technique That Has Changed

Look at old film of golfing greats from the past—Ben Hogan, Gene Sarazen, even greats in the 1960s—and you'll notice a lot of wrist action on a putt, wrist action that usually finished with a "pop" of the ball. Many golfers today think that such a technique is fine for slower greens (most greens were slower a generation ago), but today's faster greens require almost no wrist and more of a pendulum swing from the shoulders. While this change in technique may very well be warranted, all it will take is one successful pro using the old-style wrist action, and a wave of golfers will change their strokes once more.

Finding the Right Grip

Find a grip that's comfortable. Some teachers suggest a grip in which the palms of each hand face each other, with the thumbs of both hands on top of the club. Most teachers direct a beginner to a specific grip the particular teacher has found to be successful. However, there are scads of effective putting grips.

Here are a few grips to toy with. Begin with your standard golf grip, the one you've become comfortable with from tee to green. Next, try a reverse, overlap grip. Put the pinkie of your bottom hand on the club and drape the index finger of your top hand over the fingers of your lower hand. Then, try a cross-handed grip. Take your top hand and put it below, and place your bottom hand on top.

There are excellent putters using variations of all three of these grips. Don't be persuaded by any golfer at the local club (and not even the pro) who claims that a specific grip is the superior putting grip. The most comfortable grip is the right grip for you. However, if there's a common thread in every grip, it's a light touch. The consensus is that a light touch on the putter is the right touch, so hold your putter as lightly as possible.

FACT

Any grip that allows you to maintain a putter head square to the line of the stroke, helps you to maintain a stroke on the target line, and helps you control the speed of the putt is a candidate for the right grip.

Rocking the Shoulders

Most of the putting motion comes from the shoulders. Imagine that your arms, coupled with the shaft of the putter, unite to become the arm of a pendulum. The head of the putter is the weight at the bottom of the pendulum. Your shoulders provide the energy to swing it. The less the wrists are involved, the straighter the stroke from the shoulders and the steadier and more consistent its motion and speed.

The Right Stance

Much of the discussion about putting grips can be restated about a putting stance. There are certainly ideals about balance and posture that can be helpful. Many of golf's top teaching gurus suggest standing tall over the ball, but you'll also find outstanding golfers who hunch over the ball. Find a stance that is comfortable and easily repeatable without a lot of thought—a stance that, like the right grip, helps you keep the swing of the putter on the right line.

Keys to Accuracy

Putting is really a simple act. Pick your line, decide on speed, and then make sure the putter is square at impact. If your line and speed are correct, and the putter is square at impact and gliding directly down the target line, the putt will go in. Simple.

Putter Head Square at Impact

Since you don't cock and release your wrists when putting, keeping the club head square at impact is an easy task. Line the putter head up, and it should never turn throughout the stroke. Of course, the longer the putt, the longer the stroke. The longer the stroke, the more the toe of the putter will slide open on the backswing and closed on the follow-through. A good stroke coming predominantly from the shoulders will usually have the head of the club perfectly square for at least six inches behind and in front of the ball.

FACT

Some of the best putters accelerate the putting stroke through the ball; others keep the speed of the stroke more or less constant. There's probably an exception out there somewhere, but it's unlikely you'll ever find an excellent putter who decelerates the club toward impact. Plan your putt, speed, and line, and then have confidence to putt your plan.

Pendulum Swing from the Shoulders

Keeping the shaft of the putter on line may prove a bit more difficult. Concentrate on rocking the shoulders back and forth in the same plane. The shoulders don't turn so much as they rock, like the rung of a rocking chair. If your body isn't properly aligned, the pendulum arm may cross the target line rather than trace it.

You do see some golfers who stand with an open stance, some who hunch or stand too upright, and some who have very unorthodox putting strokes. Perhaps you, too, will develop an unorthodox, but successful, putting stroke. However, the easiest way to early putting success is to keep the stroke simple with hands that don't wiggle and shoulders that rock on line with the target line every time without a conscious thought.

FIGURE 12-1

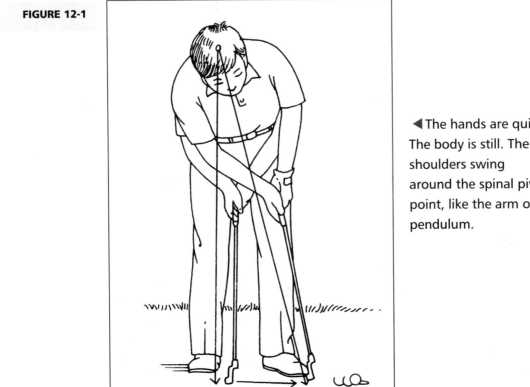

◀ The hands are quiet. The body is still. The shoulders swing around the spinal pivot point, like the arm of a pendulum.

Rules about Marking Balls

The rules of golf specifically state that any time you lift the ball on the green, the ball must be marked. Some people use ball markers, some use small coins. Mark the ball by placing a marker directly behind the ball in line with the hole. The ball must be returned to this exact position.

Sometimes it happens that your ball's lie on the green places your ball on the putting line of a golfer who is away. In that case, the marker for that ball won't be placed directly behind the ball. Instead, you place the putter head next to the ball, perpendicular to the target line, and place your marker behind that putter head. Once the person who was away has putted, go immediately to your marker, and reverse the process.

Etiquette on the Greens

Golf is a game of rules, honor, and etiquette. Practically every year a pro in a tournament realizes he or she has done something not allowed by the rules and declares a penalty on him- or herself. No one else saw it, but the pro knows it, and the pro's honor demands that he or she declare the penalty. Winning not only means playing by the rules, but winning requires that the golfer does everything possible to avoid interfering with an opponent's efforts to play his or her best.

Pick Up Your Feet

Beginners may damage the greens with their golf shoes and not realize they've done something inappropriate. If you don't pick up your feet when you walk on the green, you'll scuff it. You'll tear some of the grass, pull up some roots, and otherwise leave a damaged area that will affect the roll of a putt in ways not easily read.

An even worse scuff mark is created when a golfer reaches into the bottom of the cup to retrieve the ball and turns away, twisting the foot that's on the ground rather than lifting it. As a result, right next to the hole, in the area where other putts will be slowing and prone to the affects of blemishes in the green's surface, is a spot that will unfairly advantage a wayward putt, or disadvantage an accurate one. The problem with scuff marks is that the rules of golf don't allow their repair unless a commissioner of the tournament gives permission.

Don't Stand in an Opponent's Putting Line

Standing on another player's putting line is another common mistake. It's easy to get busy studying the green, preparing for your putt, and forget about the path other balls will take to the hole.

After holing out, don't reach in the cup for your ball without a thought for where you're placing your feet. A footprint crushing the grass and compacting the soil will cause a rolling putt to shift in its course a small amount. Not much perhaps, but a precise putt could very well be altered.

Flag Stick Damage

Take care pulling the flag stick from the hole. Don't yank it out. And don't reach lazily from an angle and pull it out. Lift it straight out from the hole. Sometimes lifting the flag out at an angle will cause the whole cup to lift with it. More often, the stick being pulled at an angle damages the precisely cut hole in the grass and dirt. This means that some balls that shouldn't fall into the cup will, and some that should, won't.

Take care where and how you lay down the flag. Don't plop it down on the green. Take it to the side of the green and place it down on its side. Allowing it to fall to the green will leave another small indentation, meaning that golf balls rolling on that green for many rounds to follow won't be rolling as true as they ought.

After you've holed out, don't be impatient. Wait for the rest of your group to finish putting before heading to the next hole. You're playing the game not just against each other, but together. Ⓔ

Chapter 13

Troubleshooting

There isn't a single golfer in history who has mastered the game. Every golfer finds that there is always some aspect of his or her game that's off the mark. If an "off the mark" part of your game is painfully apparent, don't worry. This chapter will help you determine the cause and the cure for the problem.

A Novice's Definition of Hook and Slice

Beginners shouldn't concern themselves too soon with the real definitions of hook and slice (shots that curve across and away from the target lines), because the obsessive beginner will be driven nuts. Instead, shift the definitions slightly so that hooks and slices have to do with balls that curve away from the target line and into the rough. As a beginner, you can give yourself a wider margin of error and deem it acceptable.

There are a pair of characteristics that describe a hook or a slice. The first characteristic has to do with the spin imparted on the ball by the club face. For a right-handed golfer, the club face imparts a counterclockwise spin to create the hook, making the ball curve left. For a slice, the club face of a right-handed golfer strikes the ball creating a clockwise spin, and the ball curves to the right. The second characteristic is that hooks and slices are, by definition, out of control.

FACT

A draw and a fade have the same spins as a hook and slice respectively, only to a less excessive degree. Draws and fades are controlled and enable you to send the ball where you want it to go, using spin to get it there.

Correcting a Hook

Troubleshooting begins with a piece-by-piece examination of the three main ingredients to the ball strike: swing path, club face angle, and arm/wrist position at impact. Certainly, there could also be a variety of contributing factors such as improper setup, faulty ball position, or poor timing during your body's uncoiling, but all of these contributing factors are on display in swing path, club face angle, and arm/wrist position at impact.

Swing Path

The first thing to check is swing path. On swing path, you can probably treat yourself in the comfort of your own backyard instead of going to a golf shot doctor. Using plastic golf balls or no golf balls at all, set up a video camera directly along the target line and well behind the range of the swing. It might even be a good idea to put a target line on the ground. Hit some balls. From the video camera's perspective, you should be able to identify quickly whether your swing is approaching the ball from the inside (the correct approach) or from the outside.

Your swing should intersect the target line at just the point where the ball rests. If your swing intersects the target line early and then strikes the ball, your inside-out swing becomes an outside-in swing. If you're confident that your swing path is correct, look at the angle of the club face.

Club Face Angle

If the swing path is right, go back to your video tape. If the club face is closed at impact, the golf ball will hook. A slight early release of the wrists can cause a closed club face. Cupping the left wrist near the top of the backswing can cause a closed club face as well. Cupping the wrist—drawing the back of the hand and the top of the forearm closer together when cocking your wrist—will often prevent you from returning your club face to a square position at impact.

Arm/Wrist Position at Impact

Arm/wrist position at impact will have a lot to do with the club face angle, but while the club face angle may be altered anywhere along the swing, all your arms and wrists have to do is return to their position at set up. It's as simple as that . . . and as difficult. Still, getting the correct "program" in your head begins to straighten out the problem. Even though you're swinging the club, a high-speed camera will show that the best ball strikers have their arms and wrists straight at impact, and in an identical position at setup.

ALERT!

Your whole body won't return to the same position, so don't chase your setup. At impact, the hips are rotated forward, and the weight has shifted and is still shifting forward. Only the arms and wrists will be in their setup position at impact. The rest of the body is out in front, clearing the way for the speed that the arms and wrists will generate.

Correcting the Slice

Eighty percent of all golfers have problems slicing the ball. Slices can be produced by movements opposite to those discussed with hooks: an outside-in swing, wrists not cupped but bowed, and club face open. Most of the time, when beginners and high handicappers have problems with slicing the ball, it's due to use of a baseball swing.

A baseball swing uses wrist action more quickly, throwing the club off the swing path and producing an outside-in swing. A baseball swing also rotates the shoulders much more horizontally, further contributing to the outside-in swing. Of course, even if you've never swung a baseball bat, you may still have difficulty with slicing. If so, try to first identify what's causing the problem.

You can try the video solution mentioned earlier, or use a person standing behind you, looking straight down the target line to determine from which side of the target line your club actually strikes the ball, and which direction it travels after it strikes the ball. If the club is in path, yet you're still producing a slice, something is happening at impact with your hands or during your release.

Remember, at release your hands and arms should have returned to the setup position. Hands and arms should be straight, with the back of the front hand aimed at the target.

Once you've determined the problem, drill yourself until you're able to correct the faulty position or swing. If you do enough drills and program your mind to set up and swing correctly, pretty soon you won't be having as much trouble with hooks and slices.

ESSENTIAL

Straighten out the swing path first, the angle of the club face second, and position of hands and wrists at impact last. Once you can repeat a good swing over and over, diagnosis of club face angle and position of arms and hands is easier. Once you can repeat swing and club face angle, you can work on the proper release and find straighter shots with more power.

Stopping Tops

If you top the ball (hit the ball above its center), don't feel as if you're alone out there. This is a common problem for many beginners, and even some regular golfers. The causes of topping shots include: moving the fixed axis, improper weight shift and shoulder turn, and looking up too soon.

Maintain the Fixed Axis

By now, so much of what you're learning is linked to so much of what you've already learned, but some things are necessarily redundant. You do want to improve your game, don't you?

The basic swing motion introduced the concept of the fixed axis around which the golfer swings. The torso tilt sets and maintains the fixed axis. Certainly there are some golfers who bob and weave, yet somehow manage to realign the tilt of the spine just before impact, but this usually comes with a great loss of power. Keep the swing motion as simple as possible. Maintain a stable axis, and you'll have better power and limit your topped shots.

FACT

A fixed axis that is lower at setup and raised at impact raises the low point of the swing. You'll top shots with a raised axis because the swing's low point will be too high to strike beneath or in front of the ball.

Weight Shifted Too Far Forward

More of the basic swing motion, again. If you find that your weight has shifted toward the outside edge of your front foot, your weight has overshifted. This can happen when you try too hard to make your weight shift, or when you exaggerate the initial hip action at the beginning of the downswing. The good news is, once you've grooved your swing motion, you'll probably notice the smallest shift toward an excess and make the necessary minor adjustments without even thinking.

How does excessive forward weight shift cause a golfer to top the ball?
Shifting the weight too far forward shifts the low point of the swing forward. This means you'll hit the ball with the bottom of the club on the way down, well before the swing's low point, thus topping the ball.

Looking Up Too Soon

This is usually the first reason others give you for topping the ball. Sometimes it is the reason, but it's third in the list of most frequent causes, not first. Usually a golfer taking a premature peek at the target isn't *lifting* the head to take a look, he or she is *turning* the head to take a look. When you turn your head to take a look, you don't raise the low point of the swing by lifting the fixed axis. You also don't move the low point forward as happens when your weight shifts too far forward. Instead, you move the low point of the swing back.

When you turn your head too soon, chances are excellent that you'll change your shoulder rotation, raising the front shoulder a little and dropping the back shoulder. The swing's low point will now come several inches to perhaps a foot behind the ball, and your club will strike the ground and bounce, topping the shot. From now on, if you see that divot in the ground behind the ball, you'll know why it happened and what to do about it.

When Your Club Hits the Ground First

Maybe you're not topping the ball, but the discussion about hitting behind the ball reminds you that you often do that. You'll get the ball into the air, so you know you aren't topping it, but a shot sailing into the air after you've plowed a furrow into the ground probably won't travel much farther than a topped ball.

There are three causes to hitting behind the ball, two of which will sound exceedingly familiar. One will be new, but see if you can figure it out before you read about it.

Lowering the Fixed Axis

This cause is logical. If you top a shot by raising the fixed axis, then you hit behind the ball by lowering the fixed axis. Sometimes a beginner who has heard about hitting down on a ball will drop the torso toward the ball just before impact, the same way a lumberjack delivers an ax to a felled log. If the golfer has also raised the axis before lunging downward, the golfer just might get lucky and strike the ball at the moment the axis returns to setup and before it continues its free fall toward the ball. But, this golfer will never be able to repeat this movement consistently.

Rotating Your Head Prematurely

You can dig into the ground behind the ball and still hit it straight for the same reason that many such shots are topped: You rotate your head toward the target prematurely. This raises the front shoulder and lowers the back shoulder, making the swing's low point come a few inches too soon. The more subtle your head rotation, the less likely the topped shot. You'll probably be hitting the ground closer to the ball, and the club won't have as good a chance of bouncing. What you'll notice is the divot begins an inch or two behind the place where the ball was. If the ball strike was closer to perfect than that, you'll notice the loss of distance on the shot—you hit it fat (the club hit behind the ball, taking a divot before striking the ball).

FACT

A proper swing will lift your head plenty quick enough. Keep both eyes on the ball as long as possible, and your shoulder rotation will naturally turn your head toward the flying ball and the target shortly after impact.

Have You Guessed the Third Cause?

If you have, congratulations, you're well on your way to taking control of your game. This reason is just as logical as the rest: The ball position is too far forward. Everything about your swing may be perfect, with the swing's low point occurring about two inches inside the heel of your front foot, but, if the ball is resting in front of that position, you'll hit the ground first.

In the same way, when teeing off with a driver or with a long iron, if you want to sweep the ball up into the air just after the low point and the ball is too far forward, you'll either hit a low shot that won't clear the hill in front of you, or you'll top it. When using the driver off the tee, the ball should be positioned between the big joint of the big toe and the tip of the big toe itself.

If you're consistently hitting fat shots, readjust the ball back in your stance a fraction of an inch. It may be that your swing isn't well grooved, and the low point is fluctuating a little. Or, perhaps you're just lining up the ball a little far toward the front foot.

FACT

Hitting down on the ball requires knowledge of the swing's low point, not manipulation of torso, axis, or swing arc. Sometimes to take full advantage of a high-lofted club, you can position your stance so that the ball rests perhaps three inches, rather than the usual two, behind the heel of the front foot.

Raising a Low Trajectory

Many golfers, including some very fine pros, characteristically hit shots that are a little too low. If all your shots are low, your problem is likely caused by one of three reasons: posture, swing plane, or club shaft.

Posture

If you're bending your knees a little too deeply, you'll probably hit the ball too low most of the time. Chances are that in order to maintain your balance with more knee bend, your torso is more upright and farther away from the ball. The result is going to be a shallower swing plane. In other words, you won't be able to hit down as much on the ball with a flatter swing.

Another way to get a too-flat swing from posture is to bend toward the ball with the torso tilted too steeply. Excessive torso tilt sends a signal to some golfer's brains that they're too far over the top of the ball, and they'll instinctively compensate by flattening the swing.

Swing Plane

Even a golfer with good setup posture will have a tendency toward a certain swing plane. You can work to change swing planes, making one that's steeper feel more natural. A good rule of thumb is that a swing plane less than forty-five degrees is too shallow, and one more than forty-five degrees is too steep.

Troubleshooting can become a little overwhelming to the beginner. If you're panicked about the faults in your game, first know that you aren't the only one. Even great golfers have to troubleshoot their games. Second, remember that you're out there to have fun. Don't get so serious about the game that you lose sight of that fact.

Club Shaft

Always examine your posture first. Bad posture will not only impact trajectory, it will rob you of distance on most shots. Always examine swing plane, next. If it is too flat, you can raise your swing plane toward forty-five degrees and hit it consistently.

Assuming your posture is correct and your swing plane is on target, it's possible that the shaft of your club can make a difference in ball flight. A good golfer can take a club and make the ball fly the way he or she wants. Even so, the very best will be at their very best with a shaft flex that allows them to swing naturally according to their strength, size, flexibility, and the club-head speed they're able to generate. If you're confident about your swing, don't be suspicious if the pro at the club watches you awhile and suggests you test for a different shaft flex. But don't fall prey to equipment manufacturers who claim to design clubs and balls that help golfers hit shots with a "pro" trajectory. Save your money.

Lowering a High Trajectory

To lower a high trajectory, reverse what you've learned above about posture and swing plane. And, once more, club shaft could make a difference, too.

Posture

Stand up too straight and you'll probably hit the ball on a swing plane that is too steep. Taller golfers are more prone to shots with excessively high trajectories. However, even shorter golfers can swing the club too steeply if they stand too tall or stand too close to the ball and ignore the rules of a good setup and swing motion.

Swing Plane

Even with good posture you can make a swing plane too steep. Resist the temptation to think about hitting down on the ball. If you mastered the basic swing, you'll do that repeatedly, and well. Some golfers who deliberately try to steepen the plane of the swing find they develop other problems, such as an outside-in swing leading to pulled shots (shots that head undesirably to the left on impact) and slices. Work to groove a natural swing that takes away the club on the backswing and delivers the club on the downswing at forty-five degrees for optimal height and maximum carry.

FACT

Making slight changes in the position of the ball has the effect of shallowing your swing or making it steeper. A ball positioned a bit more forward "shallows." A ball positioned a tad back "steepens" the swing plane. Don't chase trajectory by manipulating the ball. Fix your swing. Then, a little tweaking will make you an artist.

Club Shaft

Don't pursue a change of trajectory by changing club shafts for a quick fix. It may help you if you have shafts with more flex or less flex, but you can learn control over the ball with the clubs you have. If you learn control first, then finding the right flex will help your entire game all the more.

Altering the Swing's Low Point

To talk about the low point of the swing in the this context is not necessarily a topic for beginners. Indeed every golfer has to be mindful of the swing's low point, and you've had the term drilled into your head plenty so far. Once you get confident control over this portion of the swing, you can alter the trajectory of the golf ball by making minute changes to the low point—almost mental changes—at setup. Instead of having to manipulate the position of the ball, you can manipulate the low point.

Think of it like this. Strike the ball at its equator or slightly below, and the trajectory for the given club you're using will be lower than normal. Strike the ball below the equator—keep the low point at or slightly in front of the ball—and you will maximize the loft of the club you're using.

Your golf game will never be perfect—no one's ever is. But if you dedicate enough time and practice, there will be those glorious days when you're in command of your every shot, almost by willing it. (E)

Chapter 14

Lies and Hazards

Golf courses are designed to reward, punish, and make you think. Understanding lies and how to escape from difficult situations will improve your shot making and your scoring. This chapter will give you the know-how you need to make your way through the course and overcome the obstacles in your path.

Downhill Lies

The real danger for a golfer who is addressing the ball with the front foot lower than the back foot is hitting the ground behind the ball. This can happen for a couple of reasons. First, subconsciously, you may think that with the ball aiming downhill, you must lift it to get it into the air. But deep in your golfer's heart, you already know that's wrong. Second, and more important, your golfer's heart is telling you to do the right thing—maintain your basic swing motion—but you can't make it happen on a slope.

FIGURE 14-1

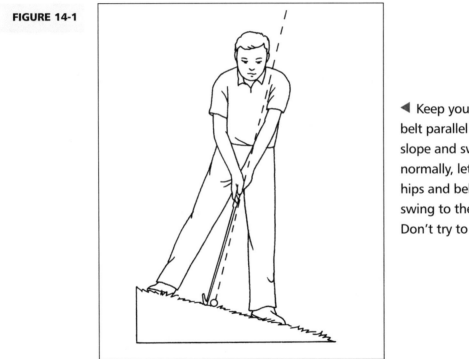

◀ Keep your hips and belt parallel to the slope and swing normally, letting your hips and belt match the swing to the slope. Don't try to lift the ball.

The way you maintain the swing you've worked so hard to develop is to adjust your hips. Align your belt so that it's parallel to the slope. Then use your basic swing motion. This is easier said than done, but with practice, you'll learn to adjust your weight shift and balance to make it happen. The key is the alignment of the hips.

Once the hips are aligned, hit the ball normally. The ball should fly off the ground with a loft similar to the loft of that club on flat ground, only this loft will be relative to the slope. In practical terms, it means you're likely to get more roll hitting a seven iron from a downhill slope than off flat ground.

FACT

There are those who say align your shoulders with the slope. This advice is well and good, perhaps, but the hips connect the feet with the shoulders. Your feet are already parallel to the slope. Aligning your hips with your feet makes it easier to tie in your shoulders. Think shoulders first, and you might forget your hips.

Uphill Lies

When hitting from uphill lies (lies on which your front foot is higher than your back), the same rule about keeping your belt parallel to the slope applies here. Aligning your hips parallel with the slope will help you to align your shoulders parallel, too.

FIGURE 14-2

◀ Remember to keep your hips and belt parallel with the slope, and swing with the slope.

Hitting the ball off an uphill lie presents a pair of problems. The first problem occurs if your hips aren't parallel to the ground. In which case, you'll have a good chance of hitting the ball, but you'll probably take a lot of turf with the shot. That means there will be a great reduction in distance. Of course, the way to prevent this is to be certain your body parts are properly aligned parallel to the hill.

ALERT!

An uphill lie will exaggerate the loft of the shot. To get the same distance as you would off flat ground, consider a longer, less lofted club for the shot.

The second problem, however, can occur *because* you're properly aligned. Aligning properly is the first step to a good shot off downhill and uphill lies, but on an uphill lie, shifting your weight to your front foot is much more difficult. If you don't shift your weight to your front foot, chances are good that you'll pull the ball. For a right-handed golfer, this means hitting the ball on a straight line well left of the target line. Proper weight shift is always important for good shots.

Playing the Ball below Your Feet

You're already thinking "basic swing motion"—excellent. But an adjustment must be made with the weight. With the ball lower than your feet, you'll have to bend your knees more to get the club on it. More knee bend means the body is in the way more.

The Illness and the Cure

Think back to the discussion about moving the hips or clearing them on the downswing to help keep the speeding arms and hands on the swing path. With more knee bend, you've got more body in the way of the swing. This means you'll have a tendency to push the ball because you're trying so hard to maintain your inside-out swing that the swing path never aligns with the target line; it only crosses it and keeps going.

Or, even more likely, your bent knees throw the swing path out of line, and you strike the ball with an outside-in path, slicing it. Either way, there's a strong tendency to send the ball to the right, wide of the target, when the ball is below your feet.

FACT

Pushing or slicing is prevalent when the ball is below your feet. Consider changing your target line from directly at the hole—assuming that's where you want the ball to go—and aim several degrees to the left of the target. That way, you help take the errant shot, which goes far right, out of play.

You've probably already anticipated the cure. Keep your weight back into the slope. This will help you to maintain good posture, and help keep your knees from altering the intended course of the shot.

FIGURE 14-3

◀ Maintain your balance by leaning back into the hill. Your swing path will be steeper than normal.

A Warning

Take care with your caution about weight, alignment, and ball strike. You could double-cross yourself. This can happen to a beginner, but it's more likely to happen to you once you've had some experience and know how to compensate for the push/slice tendency. Don't let the heel end of the club strike the ground before the sole of the club. If it does, you'll have double-crossed yourself. If the heel strikes first, you could wind up shanking the ball, sending it way to the left. Or, the heel will close the club face and you'll pull the ball (same direction as a shank, different cause).

When the ball is below your feet, keep your weight into the slope and align the club at address so that the sole of the club will hit the ground before the heel. Also, aim a bit left of your intended target.

Playing the Ball above Your Feet

When playing the ball above your feet, the tendency is to pull the ball—hit the ball on a straight line to the left if you're playing right-handed. To hit the ball solidly, your weight needs to shift toward the balls of your feet. Just like hitting a ball from below your feet, you lean into the hill. However, in order to keep good balance, this time it means leaning toward the ball rather than away from it.

Any time you aren't on reasonably level ground, your body weight shift is less than automatic. Work on your weight shift. Make sure you duplicate the basic swing motion as closely as possible. The lack of weight shift is one of the key reasons the ball wants to scoot left.

However, the ball doesn't *always* want to scoot left. If you don't align the sole of the club so that it's parallel to the uphill slope, you run the risk of having the toe dig into the hill on a less than perfect shot. This will open the club face and send the ball further up the slope. Align the sole of the club parallel with the uphill slope to keep the ball from going several degrees right of the target.

FIGURE 14-4

◀ Lean into the hill for good balance. Your swing will be shallower from this lie.

To take most of the danger of a pushed shot out of play, aim a little to the right of your intended target so that if the ball goes straight or slightly left it will be nearly on line, and a ball pushed left will still give you a playable shot.

Playing from the Rough

There's no need to panic every time the ball misses the fairway and lands in the rough. The rough at many golf courses doesn't dignify the word "rough." On courses that have an intermediate rough (the area adjacent to the fairway), it may be nothing more than pristine fairway allowed to grow a couple of inches tall. On the other hand, a ball landing in tall grass, grass that's four inches or more, presents plenty of complications for golfers of every ability.

FACT

The best general rule for hitting a shot from any kind of rough is to swing more vertically. Alter the club path a bit so that it comes down toward the ball from a steeper angle. This will help reduce the amount of grass trapped between club face and ball, and improve your odds of hitting the ball more accurately.

Hitting from Intermediate Rough

So the management has narrowed the fairways a bit by allowing the sides to grow a little taller. One punishment the intermediate rough delivers to all golfers, regardless of ability, is that a ball rolls significantly less far in the intermediate rough than on the fairway. In effect, the better amateurs may be hurt a bit more for the reduced roll, because they're likely to have played enough golf to have planned which club and what type of shot they expect to play next, given a good landing and a typical roll in the fairway. The intermediate rough will cause a ball to fly. This means that just enough grass may get in between the club face and the ball to reduce some spin and send the ball farther than that same club usually sends it.

QUESTION?

What two elements of a golf shot does a golfer lose most control over in the rough?
Distance and trajectory. Both distance and trajectory depend not only upon a consistent swing motion, but also on how cleanly the ball is struck. Grass coming between the club face and the ball can make a shot go farther and lower than normal, or grab the club head and apply brakes to the club-head speed.

Let's say you are developing a good game and have discovered you can count on your seven iron for 150 yards every time, and that's just what you need now to reach the pin. What should you do if you think the grass may send your ball 160 yards—enough distance to roll off the green and into a bunker? The quick answer is to use your eight iron. The problem is that sometimes out of the intermediate rough, ball strike is so clean, it's like hitting off the fairway. If that happens, then you won't reach the green; you'll land in the bunker in front.

The keys to success out of the intermediate rough are practice and experience. By learning to steepen your swing and hit consistently, you'll probably still be able to use your trusty seven iron because the steeper swing path will reduce the amount of grass on the club face and send the ball out with a higher loft. That's a long way of saying that with work you'll learn to reduce problems from the intermediate.

Hitting from the Jungle

The rough at some courses is just weeds and sparse grass, as often as not giving a player a decent lie to shoot from. But grass above four inches is nasty. It will grab your club and alter your shots. It absolutely demands a more vertical swing.

If you're physically strong, with a great swing generating superior club-head speed, you may not be able to hit the kind of shot that will land your ball ten feet from the pin, but you'll get out of the jungle stuff consistently. But for weaker golfers, or golfers who generate less club-head speed, the deep rough can be severe punishment for an errant shot.

First, you might not get the ball out of the rough on your first (or second, or third!) shot. Beginners and high handicappers often don't get the club to the ball fast enough in the high grass before the movement of the grass causes the ball to settle down a few fractions of an inch deeper. The result is that balls in the deep rough are often struck above the equator, meaning you topped it. It may scurry along several feet, or it may settle down deeper an inch or two in front of the last shot. Or, with luck, it may shoot down off the ground and pop up, settling on top of the grass for your next shot.

For beginners and high handicappers, don't think shots to the green, think escape to freedom. Don't think distance, think steep swing path. Resist the temptation to do anything but get the ball out of trouble. Take a club with a lot of loft—for instance, a wedge with a heavy head to help compensate for a lack of club-head speed—and move the ball back in your stance a little to ensure a steep angle on the club as it meets the ball. Hit the shot with a full swing. Don't overdo it and risk poor swing mechanics. Hit it as you have practiced to hit a full shot.

As for aiming the ball, the shortest distance out of the rough and onto the fairway may be best. If the fairway is narrow and you're swinging confidently, it's possible you could fly the ball out of the rough, over the fairway, and into more trouble. You'll have to decide, but often the best play is to aim down the fairway slightly. The angle will increase the ball flight necessary to clear the rough by only a few yards, yet it will increase greatly the distance the ball can carry toward your eventual destination without landing you in even more trouble.

ALERT!

Hit the right shot. The right shot out of the rough is the shot that gets you out of trouble. Don't second-guess the shot with the wedge that put the ball out on the fairway but didn't advance the ball toward the flag. If it got you out of trouble, it was the right shot.

From Behind Trees

Creative shots are probably more tempting from behind trees than from any other predicament on the golf course. The reason often has to do with the lie. A tree's shade tends to discourage the growth of grass and thick weeds underneath the canopy of leaves, or the tree is out on the fairway. Either way, the ball often rests on short grass or hard ground.

High school and college golf coaches often advise their players: "If you weren't good enough to keep your ball from getting behind that tree in the first place, what makes you think you can hit a banana slice or duck hook the ball around the tree and onto the green?" However, hitting from behind trees may be the best place for the beginner to try his or her hand at creative shot making. Even if trying to get the ball to slice seventy degrees is preposterous and out of the question, oftentimes a creative shot can advance the ball well enough to avert disaster on the hole.

Out from under Limbs

Let's say that from your lie, you see that you can advance a straight shot 150 yards toward the green and remain safely in the fairway. That shot will also leave you a pitch shot from the pin. The problem is, you usually hit a seven iron 150 yards, but a seven iron will send the ball into the overhanging limbs.

The common advice is to take a club with less loft (for this shot, probably a five iron), but experience will better instruct you. Move the ball back in your stance a little and swing away. Be sure you hit the ball, and not the ground, first. Hitting the ball first with it back in your stance will ensure that the ball comes out low. But if your divot begins before the ball, the ball may fly up into the limbs.

Another creative, but less risky, shot is to use your four iron or your three iron and play it more like a pitch and run. The ball will come out low and roll a long way. It may not be as rewarding as the first creative shot, but it's probably safer.

FACT

Hitting the ball from closer to the back of the stance means that the club face will not be quite square to the target line. The ball will tend to be to the right of the target for right-handed golfers, left of the target for lefties. Adjust the aim of your creative shot accordingly.

Hitting over the Tree

If you're far enough behind a tree, you can try to hit over it. This shot is more difficult than hitting a long, low shot from underneath the branches. Still, if you're beginning to develop some confidence in your consistent swing, give it a try. One caution: This shot works best for strong golfers. To hit the ball over the tree and get it to travel the required distance, take a less lofted, longer club, just like you did to hit under the limbs.

Confused? Picture this scenario. You've sized up the tree and know that if you hit a full wedge, you can clear it. The problem is that the green is only a nine iron away, but you don't know if your nine iron can carry the tree. Pull out your eight iron (the less lofted, longer hitting club) and open the club face so that its loft is roughly equal to the loft of your wedge. Now play your shot with the loft of a wedge and the carry of a nine iron. Don't try to lift the ball. Use your basic swing motion.

Of course, shots like these take practice. Nothing is more rewarding than deciding to hit a creative shot and hitting it right. On the other hand, nothing is more aggravating than going for it and getting into worse trouble. Decide on the shot and hit it. No regrets. Otherwise, punch the ball into the fairway, and again, no regrets.

Lost Balls, Drops, and Out-of-Bounds

There's a good chance that within a single round of golf, at least one of these three situations will happen to you: you'll lose a ball, need to take a drop, or have a ball go out-of-bounds. Learning all about these three situations will help avoid confusion on the course, speed up play, and may actually help you score better.

Lost Balls

If the course you play has lots of tall or thick vegetation in the rough, you're likely to lose a ball. If you hit a ball into deep rough, play a provisional ball. But, before you play it, tell your marker (the official scorekeeper in your foursome) that this is what you're doing. Declaring a provisional ball lets the group know that you believe the previous shot may be lost, and the shot you're playing is a substitute only if you can't locate the first one. If you find the first ball, you must play it and pick up your provisional ball.

ALERT!

Never hit a provisional ball without announcing it as such. And never declare your first shot lost without a look. To hit a provisional ball without first announcing it means you're declaring the first ball lost, and you're prepared to suffer the penalty. Then, if a member of your foursome finds your first shot, it's too late, you're stuck with the penalty.

If you can't find the first ball, your provisional ball becomes the ball in play. Of course, by losing a ball, you're penalized stroke and distance, meaning that the provisional ball now resting in the fairway is lying two.

Drops

One of the most common types of drop occurs when a ball goes into a water hazard. When a ball enters a water hazard you have three choices:

1. Take the penalty and play the next shot from a spot as near as possible to where the last ball was struck (and never nearer the hole).
2. Take the penalty and drop a ball anywhere you choose behind an imaginary line that runs from the spot where the last ball was struck to the spot where that ball crossed into the hazard (and never nearer the hole).
3. Take the penalty and go to the spot where the ball crossed into the hazard and measure a distance of two club lengths from that spot (never nearer the hole) and take a drop.

Take care to avoid a predicament that happens too often, yet is completely avoidable. If the ball doesn't splash down before your eyes, but only trickled out of view toward the water, don't assume the ball is gone and hit from the same spot. Go and check it out.

Drops Free of Penalty

There are a number of situations that allow a golfer to drop free of penalty. A ball on the cart path, on an immovable obstruction, on ground under repair, and in casual water (water pooled where it doesn't belong) are typical examples. If you're entitled to a drop, there are certain specifications for conducting the drop.

- The ball always must be dropped from shoulder height, arm extended.
- The ball must be dropped within one club length of the spot from which the golfer is seeking relief.
- Once dropped, the ball must not roll more than one club length from the area where it was dropped; then the ball is in play.
- If the ball does roll more than one club length, it's dropped a second time.
- If the ball rolls too far on the second drop, the ball is then placed within one club length of the relief area and played.

FIGURE 14-5

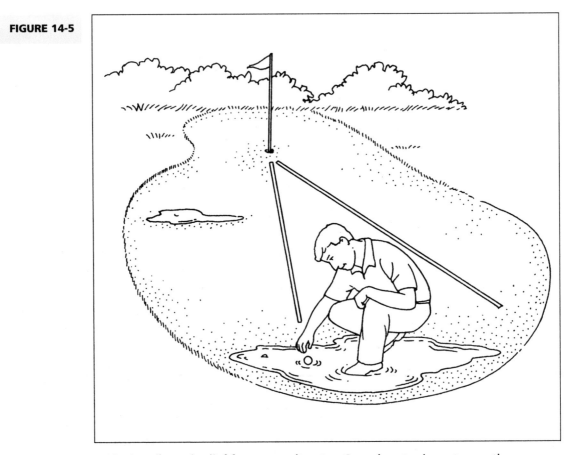

▲ You're allowed relief from casual water. Casual water is water on the course pooling where it doesn't belong. Relief means you'll take a drop within stance plus one club length, no nearer to the hole.

FIGURE 14-6

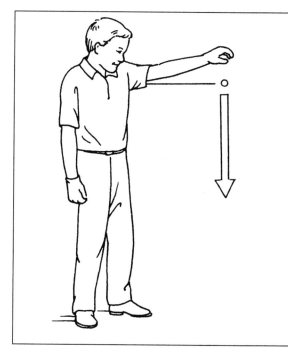

◀ With your arm fully extended, release the ball from shoulder height.

Out-of-Bounds

Some courses are so wide open it's difficult to hit the ball out-of-bounds (OB). Some are so narrow, especially those built within a neighborhood, OB is a constant possibility. It's important to be clear how to count your strokes when you hit the ball out-of-bounds.

FACT

The rules of golf can be confusing. One of the best ways to improve your knowledge of the rules governing the game is to join the United States Golf Association. Membership is currently $35 a year. You will receive a rule book and publications exploring rules and situations that can occur in a round of golf.

Imagine you are on the tee, since going OB happens more frequently there than elsewhere on a course. If you hit your tee shot OB, you tee up again. When you go to hit that next shot, you are lying three. Your first shot, the one OB, counted as one. Then you added a penalty stroke for going OB, so when you teed up the second time, it was your third shot. So now you are in the fairway, lying three.

To a beginner, the rules may seem complex. Remember, they've been evolving for over 400 years. They make the game fair, and usually, without giving one golfer an advantage over another.

Chapter 15

E Playing in the Elements

As the rain came down during the 2002 U.S. Open Championship at Bethpage State Park on Long Island, New York, one of the USGA officials was asked by a commentator if it wasn't time to call the players off the course due to the rain. To sum it up, he said "Golf is an outdoor game, played in the elements."

Wind, Ball Flight, and Club Selection

Wind isn't a problem just for high handicappers and beginners, it's a problem for every golfer who allows it to be a problem. Wind changes the ball flight. If you hit into the wind, your ball tends to balloon—go higher than the shot was planned to go, go higher than the loft of that club usually sends a well-struck ball, and go shorter. If you hit with the wind, the ball tends to travel lower, carry farther, and roll farther, too.

The Right Mental Attitude

A headwind makes all shots go shorter. That means you may need to hit longer clubs into greens, take an extra shot to reach the green, or take into consideration water and trap hazards that usually don't come in to play. You don't have to fight a headwind. Instead of swinging too hard, simply use longer clubs and hit normal shots. Make a conscious effort to relax. Once you're relaxed, swing at only a 75 to 80 percent effort, if that's what it takes for you to keep the wind from altering your swing control. Play the course and its conditions, don't let them play you.

When playing with a tail wind, the ball travels lower, farther, and rolls longer. While that can make you feel powerful off the tee, a tail wind will also change the course. More distant hazards will come into play, and wedges hit to the green may sail over the green or not sit and stop as quickly.

Too many golfers try to muscle a wind shot, defying the wind in their faces. The result is a ball flying high and often into trouble. Never muscle a shot. Wind changes the golf course and your shot selection. Embrace it and take what it gives you.

Crosswinds can move lofted shots dramatically. The experienced the golfers may be caught by surprise when they see that perfect wedge or nine iron lofted right on the target line to the pin, drift away from the flag, and find the trap.

Secrets for Determining the Wind Factor

When conditions are windy on the course, it becomes vital that you notice everything about every shot, not just your own shots, but those of the rest of your group as well. When another member of the group has honors, take the opportunity to watch his or her club selection and ball flight. If you're familiar with your playing companion's game, you can determine quickly how the wind is changing his or her distance and direction.

You've probably seen players tear off some grass and toss it into the air to gauge the surface wind. What is less apparent is what else they use to gauge the wind. They'll study the flag on the green, and they'll watch the tops of the trees. The sway of trees may be the factor most often discounted in the shot design strategies of a beginner. The wind in the trees may be coming from a different direction, or at a different speed, than the surface wind.

FACT

Your mind is your best asset in windy conditions. Be sure you take into account both the signals nature provides and the results of your partner's and opponents' golf shots when deciding what to do.

If you've ever watched a pro tournament on windy days, you likely have seen a pro with club in hand watch the shots of his or her playing companions, then walk to his or her golf bag and change clubs. The pro took all the factors into consideration, made an initial judgment about the shot, and then changed his or her mind after studying the ball flight of fellow pros whose game and ball flight the pro knows so well. Learn from this observation; it just may save your game on a windy day.

A Simple Method of Club Selection

Never become wedded to a favorite golf club and try to alter what it reliably does for you, just because it's windy. Instead, change clubs.

Assuming that the wind is reasonably constant, measure the wind as "a one club" or "a two club" wind, meaning you will change which club you use according to the strength of the wind. If the wind is deemed a "one club," then you would use a four iron when you would normally use a five iron on a day when winds are calm. If the wind is deemed a "two club," then you would use a three iron when you would normally use a five iron. If the golf course is laid out so that several holes are headed into the wind and several have the wind directly behind, measuring the wind this way becomes extremely helpful.

For example, let's say your five iron usually travels 180 yards, but the wind is in your face. Based on what you've observed and experienced on the course, you determine it's a two-club wind, meaning you take your *three* iron and hit it with confidence.

ALERT!

Even good golfers can become so adamant about what a favorite club will do for them that, despite the course conditions, they will ruin a round of golf with poor judgments about wind and club use before abandoning that club they love so well.

The same is true with a tail wind. This method won't take all the guessing out of the equation, but with experience, you'll become more accurate at gauging the wind if you gauge it by the club.

Consider Hitting Lower Shots

It's frequently the case that there's no appreciable wind on the ground, just a gentle breeze that scarcely cools the skin, but there's a one-club wind in the treetops. In this case, it can be particularly helpful to hit a low shot with a less lofted club and keep it below the wind. That way, you reduce the guess work, and place shot selection almost completely into the realm of your judgment and shot-making skill. But be forewarned: A gust can come from out of nowhere and make a great shot bad. It happens to the best players in the world.

Temperature, Ball Flight, and Club Selection

Temperature affects the flight of the ball, including its distance, loft, and spin. If you're out on the practice range one day and you seem to be tearing the cover off the ball, yet a week later you seem a whole club length shorter, maybe it's not you—maybe it's the atmosphere.

Cold and Short

The most avid of golfers play golf with temperatures in the upper thirties. The most fanatical golfers play with temperatures even lower. Even if you have no plans to play while icicles are still hanging on the trees, it's good to know that cold air shortens ball flight and reduces the spin effect on the ball.

If you've begun to develop a consistent swing, yet on a given day, shots don't seem to be flying off your club, pay attention to the temperature. While it's possible your swing is a bit off, cooler temperatures could be making the difference. Accept what the elements give you. Don't battle back by trying to swing harder. You'll be less frustrated and more successful.

FACT

Cold air is more dense than hot air. On a colder day, the ball in flight pushes through more molecules of air than it does on a hot day. The net effect is that the ball travels shorter and with less loft.

Hot Air, Hot Shots

When the air is hot, the ball travels farther and higher. But it's not quite as simple as that—hot and dry air allows the ball to travel longer and higher than hot and humid air. So it is quite possible, depending on where you live, to play golf two days in a row with the same temperature both days and on the first day get more carry and roll on your drives and more spin on your wedges than on the second day. Of course, you can't blame the atmosphere for everything. Check out your swing first. If you have a consistent swing, then it may be the humidity affecting your game.

ESSENTIAL

Heat increases the compression of a golf ball. A hotter golf ball travels farther, higher, and with greater spin. You might have noticed this effect even on a cool, sunny day, if you started a round within minutes of pulling your clubs from a hot trunk. If your body was warmed up and loose, those early holes may have yielded the longest shots of the round.

Turf Conditions

Avid golfers frequently plan vacations near courses they want to play. If it were possible to place identical courses—elevation, terrain, the works—in South Carolina and in Minnesota, those courses would play differently. The golfer traveling from South Carolina to Minnesota would face frustrations his or her northern counterpart would find amusing, and vice versa.

Fairway Grasses

The type of grass used on a golf course fairway changes the way you need to play certain shots. To keep it simple, northern states use cold-tolerant grasses, and southern states use heat-tolerant grasses. Typically, cold-season grasses are blade-type grasses that can't be cut quite as short as heat-tolerant runner-type grasses.

Hitting an approach shot into a green off Bermuda (heat-tolerant) grass will result in a shot that bounces once and spins backward. Hitting an approach from a blade-grass fairway won't produce as much backspin for most golfers. That means you have to play different types of approach shots into the greens depending on the type of fairway grass.

Imagine you're playing a course on Fripp Island, South Carolina, and your twin is playing a completely identical course in Minnesota. The temperature and humidity are the same in both places. You both have the same full wedge shot into the green. You hit that wedge, and it lands fifteen feet past the flag, just as you planned, and spins back toward the hole. If your twin hits a full wedge, too, that wedge shot off that fairway grass will bounce and probably roll off the green into the fringe.

Your twin should have managed that hole differently. Your twin could have hit a three wood instead of the driver off the tee; then the full wedge would have landed a bit short of the pin and rolled forward. Or your twin could have hit less than a full wedge.

Dew

Dew changes turf conditions. The most obvious change is that dewy grass slows a rolling ball more quickly. But as a student of the game, you're already taking that into account when you play an early morning round. Dew also changes the spin characteristics of the ball. It's good that you're in the habit of wiping off the club head after each stroke, but even so, the ball is wet. It's a hydroplane effect in miniature. Expect less spin.

FACT

You may not be able to fade or draw the ball quite as effectively in the morning dew. Conversely, if you're having trouble with slices, you may notice you slice less at that time of day.

The Four Seasons Change the Course

If you play only one course, you may not notice particular differences weekend to weekend as the seasons change. If your game has reached a plateau, the subtle changes of the course through the seasons may lead you to believe that given the time of year you are better off the tee than three months ago, or you can't hold your wedges on the green in the fall as well as in the spring. Your game hasn't changed, the course has.

The less dramatically the weather changes where you live, the less the golf course changes. A course in Key West, Florida, will change much less noticeably than a course in West Chester, Pennsylvania. But the colder the winters are where you live, the more noticeable the course changes.

The Spring Course

In spring, the fairways are softer from winter rain and snow and from alternating freeze and thaw. The ball rolls less after carry. The greens hold more approach shots, tempting you to boast about your wedge wizardry.

The balls off the tee may roll less far, but your scoring seems improved. You seem to be getting into less trouble and escaping the rough with a limited negative impact on your scoring. When a ball rolls less, an errant shot is less likely to roll into the rough, but there's also a difference in the rough in the spring. The grasses and weeds are still tender, just growing back after a winter rest. The rough is not as thick. In brief, the course plays longer, but the rough and the greens are more forgiving.

The Summer Course

Now that you've been playing regularly for a few months, you've begun to brag about how much farther you've been driving the ball in the past few weeks. The spring rains have let up and the fairways are drying out and firming up. This means that the tee shots are rolling farther. (And the air is hotter, remember?)

What you aren't bragging about, however, is that you seem to find yourself in the rough more often, and it's inflating your scores. Well, a ball rolling farther in the wrong direction will get you in more trouble, because those once tender greens of the rough are now rain-forest dense.

ESSENTIAL

When you play in the summer, look around at other holes to find sprinkling systems cooling the greens. It's very possible to play a course where the timing system has left the hole you are on dry and hard, but the pair of holes you are about to play are soft.

The thing that puzzles you the most about your game right now is that sometimes you seem able to hold shots on the green, and then on the very next hole, it hits and skids right off the green. Well, good news, it's probably not a flaky iron game after all! In the summer, the greens on your course may vary a great deal. Ordinarily, summer greens, like summer fairways, are harder, making approach shots more difficult. But greenskeepers often cool greens to ward off the effects of the heat by watering them. Then, for a while during those morning hours, the summer greens behave as if it's spring again. By the end of the day, sometimes by the end of the round, they're hard and fast again.

The Fall Course

In the fall, the temperatures are cooling and the weather is drier. The fairways are hard, and the ball carries a bit less, but may roll a little more, leaving you with similar but deceptive results off the tee: A fairway hazard you've been accustomed to carrying, or that bunker on the front of the green, now come into play. Roughs can be more treacherous in the fall than in the summer, because most of the rough is still growing and trees are shedding their leaves, adding to the danger. In addition, characteristics of ball flight can change in a single round, as temperatures warm from jacket weather to short sleeves.

The Winter Course

Depending on where you live, your course may not even be in play much of the winter. But courses in the midtemperate zone and further south certainly are. The winter brings shorter ball flight, but longer roll on frozen ground, and less danger in the rough.

Courses in the midtemperate zone usually allow golfers to improve the ball's lie in the winter by maneuvering the ball so it sits up on a tuft of grass for the next shot. But it's best to hit the ball where it lies. This will help you keep the swing's low point consistent, and raise your confidence for hitting off any lie the rest of the year.

Water Power

You've already learned plenty about the power of water. Water softens fairways, reducing the roll of a shot after carry. It softens greens, helping the ball to sit (not roll off) and to spin. And water clinging between club face and ball reduces spin characteristics on a shot.

There is another power of water, and this power beginners find hard to accept. Believe it, embrace it, learn to take it into account when you play: Water affects the roll of a putt. If there's a pond to the side of a green, the putt will veer toward it.

Rub of the Green

Things happen on a golf course over which you have no control. Sometimes what happens is good, stupendous even—the tee shot hits the paved cart path just right, bounces four or five times, then kicks back out into the fairway for an improbable 350-yard drive. Often though, the results are less than pleasing. Just chalk it up to the rub of the green.

The Immovable Objects

Your golf ball settles against a sprinkler head or a Porta-Potty. No problem, the rules of golf allow for relief without penalty. You get to drop the ball stance plus club length away. Unfortunately, it also happens that on occasion your ball hits that sprinkler head on the fly and ricochets out-of-bounds. Tough luck; you'll suffer the penalty. Conversely, you send an errant shot out-of-bounds where it hits a car and flies back in bounds, becoming your best shot ever. It's just the rub of the green.

Critter Interference

Some local clubs that have a repetitive problem with animals may have special local rules, providing relief from certain situations; but that's not always the case. A golfer may crush a fantastic tee shot, leaving it exactly where he or she wants it, but a big bird swoops down and grabs at the ball. The playing partners notice it, too. The bird moves the ball three or four yards. No problem—rub of the green—the ball is set up even better for the next shot. Then the bird tries again, grabs the ball, starts to fly, and drops it into a pond. Sadly, the golfer must follow the rules for penalty and drop from a water hazard.

FACT

Golf balls hit deer, dogs, birds in flight, alligators, Porta-Pottys, and beverage carts. Play the shot where it comes to rest. If the shot comes with a penalty . . . hey! . . . golf happens.

Divots, Pins, and Flags

It just doesn't matter what alters a shot. When you finally reach the ball, its situation at that moment is your situation, lucky break or penalty. Sometimes a great shot rolling across the green strikes the pin and rebounds a long distance away. Another occasion may bring a poor pitch shot racing seven feet off the ground across the green only to be grabbed by the flag and dropped straight into the hole below. It doesn't matter what might have been, all that matters is what is.

Where the rules of golf probably create the most anger concerns divots. If you land in a divot that someone forgot to replace, you get no relief. The ball must be played where it lies. That's the rub of the green.

Draw of the Mountain

Some people believe that putts break toward the nearest mountains. Others think that notion is hogwash. Regardless, take great care when reading a putt. The scenery around the green may deceive the eyes. A putt against a certain backdrop of scenery may appear flat, when in reality the particular amount of shade cast by the trees nearby or a solitary mountain looming off in the distance may give your eye a false read.

That's why it's important to walk around the green, getting a feel of the green's secret undulations under your feet, and let your eye view the situation facing the mountain (or the trees or the swell on the lip of the bunker) and face away from those objects that may distort your reasoning. Will a mountain actually distort the roll of your putt? Probably not. But a mountain, like any surrounding landscape feature, will certainly distort your perspective if you permit it. Ⓔ

Chapter 16

Club Selection and Strategy

E very club in the golf bag is designed to deliver certain characteristics to the ball you put in motion. If you rely on only a few clubs for every situation, you're less likely to develop a versatile golf game. Even so, it's important to know how to work with your ability to create a strategy on the course.

Alternative Uses for the Putter

You already know what the putter is for and how it's designed with little or no loft. However, the natural terrain of some courses invites the creative golfer to consider using the putter for functions other than rolling the ball the last few dozen feet toward the hole. There's an old golfing adage that goes: "A bad putt is better than a good pitch." There's some truth in that. A bad putt winds up eight to ten feet from the pin, which is about the same distance middling golfers congratulate themselves for their touch with a pitch shot.

The Texas Wedge

The terrain on which golf courses are built varies. In some parts of the country, more courses are flat. Presumably, the putter garnered the moniker "Texas Wedge" in the great state of Texas when some creative golfer perfected the art of rolling a golf ball with a putter the last thirty to fifty yards from the flat fairway and onto the flat green.

There are certain other features of the golf course that help to make this a viable shot: hard fairways with very short grass, and fairways with little or no elevation from fairway to green. Texas isn't the only place where such shots are feasible. On occasion you'll see great pros use a Texas Wedge at the British Open where the grass is extremely short. This shot is easily mastered probably because most average golfers practice more with their putters than with the wedge or seven iron or any other club of choice for short shots around the green.

Extreme Touch Shots

These putter uses are probably not practiced by any serious golfers, yet for a golfer with years of experience and an excellent touch, these shots just might work. In high rough at the edge of the green, a golfer can lay the putter back, creating more loft. Contact with the ball will lift the ball out of the rough and send it rolling toward the pin. The idea is to putt with some lift, aiming the club just like a putt, only clearing the hazard first.

A similar affect of lifting the ball and settling it quickly can be achieved by hooding (tilting the toe of the club toward the hole) the putter, creating negative loft. This shot can be used when the aim is to clear a small amount of fringe around the green or an indentation a few inches in front of the ball. This shot is definitely a putt—you're aiming just as you would on the green—but your intention is to clear some obstacle a few inches away and to allow the putt to roll true. A pitch could do the same thing, but getting the ball rolling early often helps it keep its line.

ESSENTIAL

Learn to use all your clubs as they are designed to be used first. But when a match is on the line, you don't want to use the club you are "supposed" to use. You want to use the club that you have confidence in. Play enough and you will develop your own bag of tricks, your own shots and techniques that fly right when the pressure mounts.

The Versatile Three Wood

Some people never pull a driver out of the bag because they can't control it. But you know that it's best to learn to work with all your clubs. Still, there are times when the three wood off the tee makes good sense—for instance, if the fairway is narrow and you need more control. A three wood should give you more control because it has more loft than a driver. More loft means less side spin, thus there is less tendency to slice or to hook straighter shots. That alone makes the three wood a viable alternative to the driver off a less than wide-open fairway.

More Than a Driver Substitute

The three wood is more than just a driver substitute. By having more loft than the driver, it becomes the ideal club for hitting off the fairway when the shot needs to be long. The loft allows the ball to get up in the air, a feat most golfers find difficult to accomplish when attempting to use the driver off the fairway as a second shot on a par five. Some golfers are so smitten with the three wood, they'll use it off the tee, off the fairway for long shots, and choke down on the shaft to hit shorter shots from a good lie.

Three Wood for a Pitch and Run

Okay, the use you've been waiting to discuss: the three wood for a pitch and run. Occasionally the three wood is Tiger Woods's choice for the pitch and run, and there's merit in the selection of this club. A three wood has about fifteen degrees of loft. The pitch stroke pops the ball into the air, but with only fifteen degrees of loft, the ball will roll a long way after it touches the green. The three wood for a pitch and run is a good choice (after much practice) for getting a ball in the air over the fringe, and allowing it to run uphill on a green.

FACT

Studies indicate that the carry of a three wood averages only about five to ten yards less than the carry of a driver. The driver's advantage is the roll after landing. Still, when the extra roll is of no real benefit, you might wish to consider the three wood for a few more tee shots.

Using a Sand Wedge Without the Sand

First, homage must be paid to the great golfer who developed the club, Gene Sarazen, one of the finest golfers ever to play the game. Sometime in the earlier decades of the last century, Sarazen welded a flange-type blade on a club, and the sand wedge was born.

Its advantage over other wedges is twofold. First, it has more loft, which helps lift shots out of the sand and settle them more gently with backspin. Second, it has a flange on the bottom, which helps the golfer to scoop the ball out of the bunker. The sole of the sand wedge is wider than the sole of other clubs, and the leading edge of the flange curves upward. In the sand, angling the club properly guides the club, just like the rudder of a ship passing though water. The sole of a sand wedge steers the club on a path beneath the sand.

A sand wedge can be used for a shorter version of a wedge shot. It provides a golfer with another full swing alternative at seventy to eighty yards. It lifts the ball high with lots of spin to help it settle down quickly on the green, or to shoot it well past the flag (if trouble is along the front) and spin the ball back. Some people pitch with the sand wedge, too.

ALERT!

A word of caution: If you're playing off a very hard surface or an area with little grass, that broad sole has a tendency to bounce on the ground. A ball struck less than perfectly by a sand wedge on a hard surface will be skulled—the blade, rather than the club face, will strike the ball.

Playing Conditions and Playing Wedges

The rules of golf dictate that you can carry only fourteen clubs in your golf bag for a round of golf. To a beginner, that sounds like a lot of clubs. It is if you're still working to gain a small amount of confidence in the standard set: three iron through pitching wedge, putter, driver, and three wood, and perhaps a five wood. You can configure your fourteen clubs any way you desire. Some golfers add a two iron, or a one iron, even. Others will add several woods with higher lofts.

Wedge Types

When you gain experience and confidence as a golfer, you'll probably find that you're quite happy most of the time with a driver, three wood (and maybe a five wood), and the usual irons. But instead of adding longer irons or more woods, you'll probably want to consider adding wedges to help with shorter shots from 100 yards in and closer.

Among their fourteen clubs, some golfers include as many as five different wedges. If you're a beginner, it's best simply to know that all wedges fall somewhere between these four types (they are in order of loft from lowest to highest): the pitching wedge, the gap wedge (so named because it fills the gap between the pitching wedge and the sand wedge), the sand wedge, and the lob wedge. Most other wedges available range in loft between forty-five to forty-eight degrees on the pitching wedge end and sixty degrees or more on the lob wedge end. And as you can guess, pitching wedges throw the ball up in the air least of the wedges but farthest, and lob wedges throw the ball highest, but carry the shortest distance.

Club Selection for a Particular Course

Unfortunately there's no hard rule for anyone to follow when it comes to which fourteen clubs to put in your bag for certain courses. As a beginner, you should stick with the typical set of clubs and add first a sand wedge, then a lob wedge. Once you've gained confidence in these three wedges, you can consider purchasing some other wedges.

Not every golfer carries five wedges, and a pro's clubs vary at every tournament. Factors that help golfers determine their club selection include: speed of the greens, hardness of the fairways, type of bunkers, length of the course, and length of the par fives and perhaps the par fours, too. Club selection for a good golfer can actually change from day to day depending on the weather or other factors the golfer uses to assess club selection.

Start simple with your club selection, gain confidence with what you have, then expand. One day, you, too, will juggle clubs based upon experienced diagnosis of the course and your ability.

Specialty Clubs

What's a specialty club? The philosophical answer is that a specialty club is any club that few people carry and some people have never seen. If this is the answer, then a seven wood is a specialty club because few golfers carry them, although for longer par threes, more golfers probably should consider one. Once upon a time a lob wedge and a gap wedge qualified as specialty clubs, but are now too commonplace to be considered as such. Another definition of "specialty club" includes those clubs marketed to help the golfer reduce slices or hooks, or hit the ball farther, or land it softer on the green. Some such clubs are legal under the guidelines of golf's regulations, other's aren't.

The best advice for any golfer remains: Master the basic swing motion and learn to use the legal clubs in your bag. After that, a special club that adheres to golfing regulations may be considered. But don't expect any specialty club to be everything and do everything for your game you dreamed it would do; after all, it will still be the same golfer gripping and ripping it.

Of course, you'd never get angry over a missed putt and break your putter, would you? But if you have a "friend" who does, suggest that the friend consider using the driver to finish out the round putting.

Bump and Run Shots

Many golfers think of a bump and run shot as the one used when hitting from beneath an overhanging branch, a shot of last resort. A better way to think about the bump and run is to think of it as a shot with low trajectory, a shot that's deliberately bumped off the ground (or landed) some distance from the hole and designed to run to the pin. Sometimes the only difference in a bump and run and a pitch and run shot is in the mind of the golfer hitting it. But, as a rule, pitches farther from the green go higher, land closer to the pin, and are struck with higher lofted clubs. And pitches closer to the green, rarely if ever, intentionally bring a mound or hill into the design of the shot.

The Long Bump and Run

Most golfers don't realize that the style of golfers' games varies in different parts of the country. On golf courses in the rolling hills of Kentucky or Virginia, a long bump and run shot is a rarity. On the wind-swept flat courses of Oklahoma and Texas, it might be considered standard. But there are times when golfers anywhere could take advantage of what a long bump and run offers. When wind threatens to knock a lofted shot off target or make its distance less controllable, or when your approach to the green from within 100 yards isn't threatened by water or sand, you could play a long bump and run. The advantage of the long bump and run is line-of-flight and distance control.

FIGURE 16-1

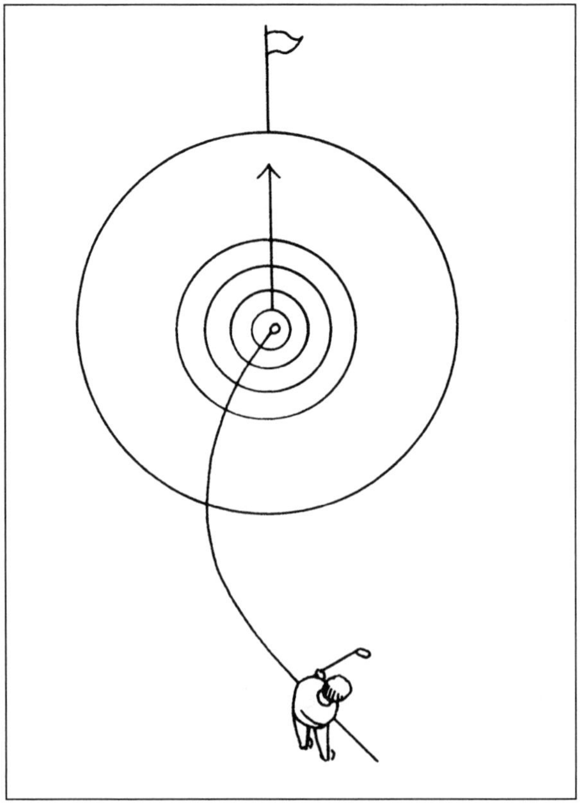

◀ Your target is the place you want the ball to land on the green and begin to run. Or, for longer shots, the place just off the green for the ball to land.

Instead of swinging a full or nearly full wedge and lofting it into the breeze or risking an off line swing, you can pull out a seven iron. Actually, what you decide to use depends on how you imagine the shot, but for our purposes, we'll use a seven iron. With your wedge at 80 to 100 yards, you'd be swinging pretty hard, but with a seven iron, something close to a half swing may be about right. You may want to move the ball back in your stance a little. Pick a target about seventy-five yards in front, a place where you want the ball to hit and begin its run to the flag or to the center of the green.

For the beginner to average golfer, the long bump and run should get you consistently on the green and occasionally close to the hole, while your high-lofted wedge shot will be consistently inconsistent.

The Short Bump and Run

Say your ball has rolled off the back of an elevated green, and the green slopes away from you. The elevation means some of the effect of loft on a shot—that flop and stop effect—is diminished. The slope away means that any shot from your direction is inclined to continue to roll.

One possible solution is the true bump and run. With a lower lofted club, you pick a target on the hill somewhere on your side of the top. The trajectory of the ball to that target will closely resemble a straight line. When the ball hits into the hill it flies up and hopefully rolls gently once it reaches the top.

Under Trees with the Bump and Run

The bump and run is a terrific recovery shot to help keep you out of worse trouble, too. If you're under that overhanging limb, thirty yards away from the green, with no hope of a traditional pitch, then bump and run. Place the ball back in your stance and send it low at a target. Even if you don't land on or stay on the green, you've taken the tree out of play, which is sure to save at least a stroke.

Don't fall in love with a certain shot and force it to mold to every situation. Instead, let your imagination, the condition of the course you're playing, and your experience determine shot selection.

From a Side Hill Lie

In an earlier discussion we talked about cautions when swinging the club on a hill with the ball above your feet (the toe of the club can dig in) and with the ball below your feet (the heel of the club can strike ground first, closing the club face). Even the swing itself from these lies can alter ball flight. Instead of a full swing with a short iron or a wedge from a side hill lie, consider a bump and run. The lower loft will send the ball longer toward the target with a shorter, more controlled swing, and you'll be using the ground to control the ball's distance.

Options from the Fairway

Where beginning golfers and high- to mid-handicap golfers are concerned, the player who hits short and straight will beat the player who hits it long and unpredictably. This is true even if the longer hitter has a better touch around the green. The reason is that the longer player will use up more strokes getting out of trouble after tee shots and will tax his or her short game to the max.

Your strategy off the tee is never to hit the longest drive. Rather, it's to send the ball toward an area that you can use to the best advantage. You want to position the ball in the fairway where you can do what it is you do best—fairway woods, short irons, middle irons.

Here's an example. You stand on the tee box of a par four, 350-yard hole. You can boom drives all day long in the 290-yard range. But you've got two problems: only about three out of ten of those drives are straight, and a 290-yard drive will leave you 60 yards to the pin, a distance that will have you guessing about which club and how hard to swing. You're considering a couple of options: a five wood out to around 220 and then a full nine iron to the green; or, a reliable 200-yard three iron, if the fairway is narrow, and an equally reliable seven iron to the green. More than one option may be viable. In which case, you will need to make your choice based upon which clubs you are more comfortable and confident with.

Every hole tests your skills and your decision making. A change in the weather, movement of the pin from the front to the back or to the side of a green, the slope on the fairway, the location of trouble, the list goes on . . . all are factors you need to consider when standing on the tee. There's no feeling more macho for a golfer than to consistently out-drive every playing partner. On the other hand, there's no feeling more smugly satisfying than to consistently play better golf than the player with a cannon for a driver.

The best question a golfer can ask before deciding on any shot is: What is *my* best chance for scoring?

Chapter 17

The Mental Game

By now you know that golf is more than just a physical game. You've learned to focus on your target, refusing to allow trouble to subconsciously alter your golf swing. But when you play golf, you're also playing with (or against) the design of the course. You're being invited to read the course architect's mind.

Becoming a Student of Great Course Design

A golf course isn't designed just to offer a view worthy of picture postcards. Golf courses are designed to offer the golfer certain choices and to take others away. Architects set up courses to be played a particular way. Their challenge is to make holes that test the skills of both the experienced golfer and the beginner, but are still fair to both.

To start you on the right path as a student of course design, we'll discuss three holes from one very fine course: a par four opening hole, a par three, and a par five.

Reading the Architect's Mind: A Par Four

This opening hole is a dog leg left, meaning the hole goes straight for a certain distance then bends to the left. The green is hidden until your ball moves past the bend. There are woods on the left, and woods and out-of-bounds on the right. The fairway slopes severely from right to left. Down the right side of the fairway about 220 to 260 yards is a fairly level mound. Whether the architect built that prominence into the surrounding slope or whether the architect designed the hole around a natural mound is not known, but it's there by intent. It's the perfect target for a landing area.

A golfer, who is a long driver of the ball, standing on the tee has a choice. The golfer could cut the dog leg by flying the ball over the corner of the woods and having the ball land on the fairway, which remains very sloped, but will leave a shot to the green of perhaps 120 yards. Or, the golfer could throttle back and land on the flat area, leaving a shot to the green of 140 to 150 yards. To cut the dog leg promises minimal reward for significant risk. To land on the mound promises a level, if longer, second shot to the green; it's the only safe shot.

For the beginner, closer tees put the target area in reach, but the trouble looming to the left and the out-of-bounds to the right are still in play. So, with one hole, this fine architect has challenged golfers at both ends of the spectrum.

Reading the Architect's Mind: A Par Five

This particular hole is the first par five on the same course. It dog legs from left to right. The holes leading up to this one were all designed for the tee shot to be safest going down the right side of the fairway.

When standing on this par five, the golfer who's not reading the architect's mind is likely to think: "To get the ball around the dog leg, I'm going to have to fade it." But this hole is designed so that a drive down the left side of the fairway is the best shot. For the better golfers and longer hitters, a drive too long could go out-of-bounds, adding to the hole's difficulty. But the reward for successfully flirting with out-of-bounds is a good clear shot allowing a golfer to go for the green in two.

For the high handicapper, a drive may not carry the ball past the dog leg. But keeping to the left will give this golfer a good angle to advance the ball a long way toward the green. On the this golfer's second shot, the out-of-bounds will come into play.

This par five, just like the par four before it, challenges both ends of the golfing spectrum. It also offers scoring opportunities (eagle, birdie) for the best golfers and scoring opportunities (birdie, par) for the worst. Same hole, but different decisions and challenges for golfers with different skills.

FACT

Sometimes a novice will wind up playing a round with an accomplished golfer. Playing a given hole, the beginner may hole out a stroke (or even more) better than the more accomplished golfer. The reason may be that the accomplished golfer failed to overcome the particular challenges/opportunities a hole posed, while the beginner faced them.

Reading the Architect's Mind: A Par Three

This same course has a rather imposing par three. The teeing area is barely elevated. Out in front and wide to the right and to the left is a lake. To go for the pin requires a carry over the water of about 200 yards. Adding to the difficulty are bunkers lining the front edge of the green, between the golfer and the hole.

At first glance off the tee, the hole looks unfair for the beginner, because that's a long carry over the water. A new golfer is already looking for the drop zone and will probably tee up an old ball, pessimistic about the shot's outcome. However, a careful survey of the hole reveals the expanse of the green. To the left of the pin, a good bit left but still looking at the green, a ball off the tee needs to carry only about 160 yards for the beginner to putt on the next shot. And, there are no bunkers protecting the green over there.

Know your game. Read the hole. Good golf courses provide the right challenges for golfers of all abilities. Make certain that you accept the right challenges given the skill of your play.

So, here's this hole's test. The good golfer will shoot for the pin, or off to the side a little to take the bunkers out of play, for a reasonable chance at shooting for birdie on shot number two. The poorer player, already challenged with the image of water that can't be erased from the player's mind, can land on the green some fifty-five feet from the pin with a long-shot chance at birdie, but with a reasonable chance for par. Same hole, tough challenges for everyone.

Learning Golf from the Four Majors

The consensus is that the four major tournaments are, in order of their annual commencement: The Masters, the U.S. Open, the British Open, and the PGA Championship. A small handful of players have won all four. But each of the major tournaments tests the world's finest golfers differently. Each major gives the golfers certain shots and takes others. The design and philosophy behind the courses used for the majors can be instructive to any golfer of any level. Just think, this is four annual weekends of televised instruction to help you play the game better.

The Masters

This course, Augusta National, was designed by one of the greatest golfers of all time, Bobby Jones. It's so meticulously maintained, you may not find a single clump of crabgrass, or any weed for that matter, anywhere, save among the tall Georgia pines. The course has very little rough. Above all the majors, this course probably rewards an excellent shot the most, as opposed to punishing a poor shot the most. The ball invariably rolls true, and great shots are rewarded with the best chances of positioning the ball on the slick greens—the slickest greens anywhere.

However, if you place the ball on the wrong part of the green, your putt may trickle, then roll, then race off the surface, and, on some holes, into the water. Wind up above the hole, and your nerves and lightest touch are tested as you tap a ball that will roll for twenty feet toward the cup.

A lot of golfers believe that the biggest test in the Masters is not surviving the glassy greens, but in shaping the shot, in the ability to hook the ball, or to draw the ball just enough to separate your shot from a good shot and making it an excellent one. Some people call the Masters a test of patience, but in a way, every major is a test of patience.

FACT

Bobby Jones won thirteen majors by the time he retired at the age of twenty-eight. While playing competitive golf, he studied mechanical engineering at Georgia Tech, got a degree at Harvard in English Literature, attended Emory University as a law student for a year and a half, and took the bar exam and passed. And you don't think you have time for golf?

The British Open

Most of the courses on which the British Open is played severely punish bad shots. The Royal and Ancient in St. Andrews may be an exception, but what's most noteworthy about British Open courses is that they sometimes punish shots that should have been great shots. A bump or a small hole in the fairway will divert a ball sending it into trouble. British Open golf demands patience and perseverance to overcome disappointments.

Wind is also almost always a key factor. Often constant, the wind on a links course (a seaside course) will cause every hole on the front to play into the wind or with a crosswind from right to left. On the back nine, the wind is completely reversed. This often demands that golfers hit low shots. Or, low shots part of the round and higher ones for another part.

The rough can be—and this is no exaggeration—completely impossible to hit the ball from, compounding the frustration of a good shot bouncing bad. And the weather is subject to change, often bringing frequent showers, meaning the course turns shots from long and fast into short shots and slow putts. Creative shot making is often demanded.

The U.S. Open

The rough at U.S. Opens is always high, deep, and thick. The ball is virtually always playable out of the rough, but the shots required are often escape shots to avoid worse trouble, not shots to score. The key to a U.S. Open is to keep the ball in the fairway and avoid the rough.

The PGA

The rough at the PGA is usually long, but perhaps the premium value of the PGA is placed on being able to hit the ball long. You've learned a lot about accuracy, and accuracy is a great asset for a golfer, but it's not the only asset. There are some courses on which a golfer whose principle asset is hitting the ball straight is at a slight disadvantage to those golfers whose accuracy is not as good, but their distance is excellent.

ALERT!

If you play only the local course, your game will adapt to the type of shots and golfing attributes that course dictates. You may find that when you play another course, even one rated easier, you have difficulty scoring. Shape your golf to fit each course.

Assessing Course Design and Planning for Play

You've already learned a bit about what goes on in the mind of a course architect, how the architect will challenge better golfers a certain way and poorer golfers another. No matter how much you learn to admire the course design of certain architect, don't forget that you have to play the course one hole at a time.

You may or may not realize that all the pros arrive at a tournament site several days early and begin practice rounds. Many of them already know the course or know that architect X does certain things certain ways. Even so, they come early in the week to take a measure of each hole, to determine what they'll do each day when it counts, to see what each hole will give them, and to see what each hole takes away.

ESSENTIAL

Don't play from the championship tees if your course has them. Play from the tees that provide you both enjoyment and challenge. As your game improves, you'll know when to begin testing more challenging tees.

Let's pretend you're about to play in a tournament. You've got your own caddie, and you've gotten some practice on the course, so you're knowledgeable about it. Follow along as we describe five holes on this course, and see if you can determine what each hole is giving you and what it's denying. By the way, the course we describe is a real one.

Hole Number One: Par Five, 520 Yards

The first hole is 520 yards, with a slight dog leg uphill. There's a bunker to the right side of the fairway, near the landing area for your tee shot. A big drive can carry over the bunker and put the long hitter in the position of going for the green in two. Out-of-bounds is treacherously close to the left side for most of the length of the hole. And, the ball has a tendency when it hits to bounce to the right.

If you aren't a big hitter and can't reach the green in two, there's a good area about 100 to 140 yards in front of the green for laying the ball up, to set up for your third shot. The green is nice and flat. The right side of the green has bunkers, which shouldn't be in play unless you overshoot the green from the left, or slice it long. The left side of the green is clear.

So, assuming you have some control over your swing, where do you hit your tee shot? And what is the green telling you? Think before you read on.

Here's the answer. Your tee shot should start down the left side. You could tee it up on the left of the teeing area, so that you aim ever so slightly away from the left-side trouble. The ball will kick to the right, so you don't want to aim to the right since the ball will wind up there anyway.

A ball on the right for a big hitter is exactly where you want to be because the flat green, with trouble only on the right, is inviting you to take out whatever club is necessary and go for the green. Being on the right already means the flight of your next shot will angle away from the bunkers on the green's right side; in fact, they shouldn't even be in play. For the shorter hitter, you should plan to land your ball between 100 to 140 yards away from the hole, depending on the club in your bag you prefer to hit. The shorter hitter can stay to the right or play the ball a little further to the left. The hole invites birdie for the long hitter, and par for the beginner.

Number Two: Par Four, 418 Yards

The second hole has a slightly elevated tee. The fairway slopes from left to right. Out-of-bounds is along the left side, and a bunker is on the right. The green is small and hard with rough tucked in close directly behind the green.

Where do you want to start your tee shot? On what side of the fairway will it end up? If you're a longer hitter, what kind of second shot will you want to play? If you're a shorter hitter, what do you want to avoid on your second shot?

Here's the answer. You'll start out your tee shot just as you did on the first hole, down the left because it will move to the right after it hits.

If you're a big hitter, you'll go for the pin with a nine iron or wedge on your second shot, unless the pin is near the back of the small, hard green. If you hit your drives short, and you must hit a longer iron to the green, you'll want to avoid going over the back of the green. This means you'll probably want to land the ball short of the green—that is, play a bump and run to avoid having to chop one out of the rough from the back side.

How are you doing so far? While it may be more convenient to simply read ahead to get the answer, it's best if you stop reading, really think about the question, and come up with your own answer first.

Number Three: Par Four, 380 Yards

The fairway drops away from the teeing area downhill, then the terrain shifts uphill. If you can hit your drives 220 to 240 yards, you'll land the ball on the upslope. There's a bunker on the right and out-of-bounds on the left and right, but still plenty of room to hit a driver off the tee. The lie is flatter down the left side of the fairway. The green is elevated, with high grass on the right. How do longer and shorter ball strikers play?

Here's the answer. The longer hitter wants to land in the flat area with the chance to use a short iron to get plenty of loft on the shot, so that the ball will land on the green and stop. The shorter driver wants to land on the flat area on the left, too. But, a longer iron to the elevated green will require the shot to hit a bit short and run. So take one club less than a shot to the pin, and plan for it to run a distance across the green. When hitting toward the high grass it's important not to be long.

Number Four: Par Three, 187 Yards

The hole is downhill all the way, meaning the hole will play shorter than the yardage. It has a big green. There's a bunker on the left side of the green, and there's thick and deep rough on the right side. The left bunker is in play if the shot is short. But a longer shot to this green means a very long putt. What do you do?

Here's the answer. To avoid the bunker and most of the rough, accept the longer putt. Hit past the pin on the second shot.

Number Five: Par Four, 407 Yards

This hole has a sharp dog leg to the right at about 300 yards. The dog leg is almost ninety degrees. Out-of-bounds comes into play on both sides, but closer on the right. From the tee there's a big tree on the left side of the fairway, which shouldn't come into play, and the fairway slopes from left to right. From the middle of the green, the slope falls away from the approach shots.

Many of the holes on this course require playing tee shots down one side of the fairway, knowing they will roll across the fairway after landing. But this green, with its slope away from the golfer from the middle of the green, requires you to consider a different question: If you're going to miss this green, do you want to miss it long or short?

Here's the answer. You need to aim for the front of the green or plan a bump and run. Everything past the middle will mean trouble.

FACT

A green sloping away from approach shots means that if the approach lands on that falling-away slope, there's hardly a chance that the ball will stay on the green. And, there's a great chance that the ball will shoot off the green with some pace.

Enjoying the Predicaments

There are times you can take advantage of holes and their design, but there are times you need to be prudent to prevent throwing away a number of strokes by trying shots the course is designed to punish. Sometimes the shot you hit is exactly the shot you planned, and the decision turns out to have been the wrong decision. Sometimes you may decide to take a chance, defying the design of the course. Maybe it works out, maybe it doesn't. And sometimes you do hit the right shot to the right place only to discover that your ball has landed in a divot. Regardless, there are two approaches to playing the game.

The-Golfing-Gods-Are-Against-Me Approach

Odd as it may seem, some people really enjoy playing golf this way. At least, they must enjoy it on some level because they keep on playing. This attitude can be cultivated when you've given up on ever improving your game—either your physical game or your mental approach to it.

This group of golfers tend to do one or more of the following: swing poorly, exercise poor club selection, read a hole and fixate on the trouble, don't read the holes at all, or are poor judges of their own ability. For example, they're the ones who hit for the hole on that par three guarded by the 200-yard lake when they should be hitting to the safe landing area. Some golfers are permanently bound to this group. A few are lured into the group by a single bad shot that leads to ruining an entire round. Every golfer has been here, but you don't have to stay.

The Is-This-a-Great-Game-or-What? Approach

The people in this group may or may not be comfortable with their present level of ability, but they accept it, at least for this current round of golf. They routinely hit consistent shots, not necessarily great ones, but consistent. They focus on the hole's possibilities for them—what opportunities a given hole provides their game. And when they do wind up in trouble, they view it as an opportunity to attempt a shot they've been practicing, or to create a shot from their "box of tools"—apply their skills, their experience, and their imagination to make something good happen.

ALERT!

If golf was full of consistently great shots and good decisions, it wouldn't be nearly as fun. If you hit bad shots or make poor decisions, just chalk it up to a lesson learned and thrive on the challenge of the game. Don't let it get to you and ruin future golfing experiences.

Saving Bogie

You've heard golfing commentators or pros when interviewed speak of saving par. They're referring to escaping trouble without it hurting the score on the hole. For example, when into the deep rough, the golfer knocks the ball out onto the fairway instead of trying for the green, hits a good approach, and one putts. However, for most golfers, and sometimes even for the pros, the best way to get out of trouble and to stay out of trouble is to think about saving bogie.

The next time you watch a pro tournament and hear about one of your favorites making six on a par three, eagerly await the video replay. Did the golfer's game suddenly turn into yours? Chances are, the pro kept trying to save par in his or her mind, even after par was no longer possible. Embrace the situation. Enjoy the predicaments. And, when you have to, take your medicine.

Embracing a Strategy to Suit Your Game

A golfer's toughest adversary in any round of golf is ego. Ego creates worse scores. For every hole on which ego made you try for a shot you shouldn't have tried, yet you found success, there are scores of holes where ego got you into worse trouble. Even on the pro circuit, the winners week after week are those golfers who know their game, remain unaffected by the strengths of their opponents, and hold their egos in check.

If you've been playing with your first set of golf clubs for only a couple of weeks, you already know some things about your golf game. You know that every time you take a full swing at the ball with practically every club, the flight of the ball is unpredictable. And you know there are three or four clubs that you can hit pretty straight every time if you only take a half swing.

If you were to venture onto the course with a foursome, should you go with that driver, hoping for the one lucky shot that sends the ball into the "Wow" part of the fairway? After all, you might get lucky. Of course, you should learn to use all of your clubs, driver included, by practicing with them first. When it comes time to play the game, play with the skills you know you have. It won't be as macho, but it will be more pleasant, and you will score better.

Never try golf shots during a round of golf that you are not prepared to hit. If everyone in your group clears the lake with the second shot on that par four or par five, and you know it's best to hit short, then hit short. Your game improves not by risk taking during a round, but by practice between the rounds.

Making Positive Adjustments in a Single Round

A pro on the practice range at Doral Country Club was overheard saying to his caddie before a tournament round something like this: "Well, let's hit a few and see how the ball flies, and we'll play the course that way." Whether he was joking or not, there was a lot of truth in what he was saying.

Monitor Your Swing

No one's swing is perfect day after day. On some days, even for those with picture-perfect swing paths, some minor ingredient is microscopically off. Pay close attention to your swing. If a golfer's natural draw curves a bit more than normal or a bit less, despite his or her best adjustments, then the golfer would be wise to work that into the game plan for the round.

Discern What the Conditions Offer

That pro could have meant that he would hit ball and make adjustments based on temperature, humidity, wind, and the roll of the ball. Then he'd make plans for how to approach certain holes. Never fight what the game is offering you on a certain day. Find your way to meld what you've got in the talent department with what the atmosphere and the course are offering.

Chapter 18

Practice, Practice, Practice!

Golf takes lots of practice. There's no getting around it. Practice helps not only to improve upon your game, but to build up confidence as well. All the effort you put into practice will manifest itself out on the course. This chapter offers some drills to help you make the most of your practice sessions.

Practicing for Near Perfection

Be honest with yourself. Are you willing to spend time practicing to improve your game? If the answer is yes, and you already put in about the same amount of time as your golfing buddies, then just an extra hour (or more) a week will move you up the foursome leader board.

For that extra hour a week, work on the strongest part of your game and an especially weak part of your game. Or, pick out an iron you find you're having to hit often in a round at the local course and hit two or three extra buckets of balls a week with just that club. Or, spend extra time sinking ten-foot putts, or chipping, or driving. The practice session is under your control, but to make the most of it, you should get to know your habits and abilities inside and out. Only you know what goes on in practice, and only you know what your strengths and weaknesses are.

Developing Technique and Confidence

Developing better technique and confidence in any single aspect of your golf game will improve your scoring, directly and indirectly. Spend extra time working on bunker shots until you discover that, nine times out of ten, landing in the sand is not a complete disaster, and you're likely to discover that you're not landing in the sand traps as much as you once did. Or, if you practice eight-foot putts until you begin to make more than your fair share, soon you won't be leaving the chip or the lag putt so far from the cup. Your new confidence in a bunker shot or in sinking that medium-distance putt also changes your mental approach to the game. To adapt a quote from Yogi Berra: "Golf is ninety percent mental, and the other half is physical."

Who Are Your Playing Partners?

If you're serious about improving your game, consider your playing partners and their abilities and practice habits. For instance, if your regular playing partners are all twenty or fifteen handicappers, your game will begin to rise to that level of play. The reason is simple enough. You acquire their golfing habits, habits likely better than those of the twenty-five handicappers you could be playing with.

Your eye will help to train your mind as you watch better, more consistent swings. In turn, your mind will help to improve your own golf swing. You'll discover that better players use better judgment in making their way around a golf course. The better players may not be long hitters, but they'll hit more consistent, more accurate—even if shorter—shots. They may lay up (hit short) instead of pulling out the big stick and going for broke. They may even lay up shorter than a poor player would deem necessary, in order to be able to get a full swing out of a club in which the better golfer has more confidence. Simply by watching, your game will improve.

Also, most of the better golfers have better practice habits between rounds. The game may be just as sociable between a foursome of players sporting a fifteen handicap as between a foursome of hackers, but the better golfers will work on their games between matches, making practice seem more a part of the fabric of the game. If practice seems normal for your playing partners it will seem normal for you, too.

ALERT!

Others may not want you around for long if your game lags way behind theirs. Understand that it has little to do with friendships, and everything to do with skill. If you can find a foursome playing at your current level and who practices for a better game, you can enjoy the ride to a lower handicap together.

Drills to Control Your Low Point

This is one of the toughest concepts for the beginner to understand: Where the club bottoms out is where the ball needs to be placed in the stance, and a golfer needs to be able to predict that low point with every swing.

This first drill probably requires that the golfer be standing on some very plush, even grass. Take out a club, address an imaginary ball, and swing. Watch where the club brushes the grass. There is the swing's low point. Typically the low point comes too far back in the beginner's stance, and is caused by releasing the wrists early or by moving the fixed axis. Drill with the swing and no ball, working to make the low point consistently about two inches behind the front heel.

You can use both of these drills to help you if you have difficulty predicting the low point. However, it's a good idea to use them every once in a while just for a checkup even if you think you've got your low point down pat.

A second drill accomplishes the same thing, only it makes the low point more obvious. Put a foot-long path of cornstarch or talcum powder, about as wide as the head of a club, in a straight line on a piece of plywood. Place a ball somewhere in the middle of that path of powder. Hit the ball. This is a means of determining very accurately the low point. Ideally the club should strike the powder at the beginning of the small round circle made in the cornstarch beneath the ball.

Drills to Stop Your Slice

The slice problem is caused by a poor swing path, an outside-in swing. Most beginning golfers have problems slicing the ball. If this is you, don't despair. Anyone can straighten their shots. You do it the same way that you get to Carnegie Hall . . . practice, practice, practice.

Use a Swing Plane Guide

You probably won't be able to pick up a swing plane guide at your local golf equipment shop. Even if you could, you might be better off befriending the golf coach at a nearby college to see if the school could make one available to you (complete with a little constructive help from the coach). There are a variety of such guides. However, they all do the same thing: help your body to feel its way through the proper swing motion. They do help, but there are other drills that can be effective as well, gadget free.

Toe to Heel Drill

This is a terrific drill for helping a golfer to get the feel of the proper swing path. First, address the ball normally. Then, pull the back foot straight off of its line parallel to the target line, roughly twelve inches straight back off the line. That will position the big toe of the back foot so that it's in line with the heel of the front foot. Now swing the club. It's still possible to swing the club outside-in from this position, but the normal swing path from this position will be an inside-out position. This drill is particularly good for getting the feel of the inside-out swing.

Hitting the Bull's Eye

Draw a pair of circles on the golf ball. The circles should be perpendicular to each other, meaning that the circles meet at the north and south poles and are ninety degrees apart at the equator of the ball. Set the ball so that one circle points directly down the target line and the other is perpendicular to the target line.

Take a permanent marker and place a bull's-eye on the inside quarter of the ball—the quarter of the ball closest to your feet. Now swing the club and hit the bull's-eye. This drill is particularly good for lower handicap golfers. Work on this drill and you can often watch your golf balls get consistently straighter over a single practice session.

FACT

While the point of practicing is to improve your game without the pressure of playing partners watching your every move, it's sometimes good to bring in a friend to assist. There are some drills that simply work better with someone else there to either offer an objective view or aid in the drill itself.

Alignment Help with a Friend's Assistance

At the practice range, stand behind the ball, sight your target (it's best to use one of the flags on the range or one of the yardage signs), pick your intermediate target, assume your setup, and freeze. Now have a friend lay down one club along the target line, and another club along your toes. Are the clubs parallel? This is a good drill to do at the beginning of any (every) practice session.

Once you get lined up consistently, repeat the drill and have your friend add a third club, across your knees. If all three lines are parallel, have the friend take that third club and place it across your shoulders. If target line, line along the toes, knees, and shoulders are all parallel, your swing path should be proper.

Drills to Eliminate Your Hook

Each of the following problems can cause a hook: an improper swing path, a closed club face, and an early release of the wrists. Sometimes more than one of these problems gang up and cause hooks.

Rope Magic

For this drill you'll need a heavy, thick piece of rope about sixteen feet long. Recall for a moment the discussion about the swing motion and parallel lines. It wasn't just feet and shoulders that were parallel. On the takeaway (when the club is moved back from the ball at the start of the swing) and on the downswing (at the point where your hands are about hip high), the club is parallel to the ground and to the target line. This position is the starting position for this drill.

ALERT!

Most beginners have problems with slices not hooks. A problem hooking is usually developed over time. Don't think you're in the clear if you haven't had this problem yet. You'll want to keep these drills in mind for future reference.

Replace your club with the end of the rope, and, in this position, pull the rope through the impact position. The rope will reflect your swing path. If you're mostly pulling the rope with your hands, the rope will indicate an outside-in path. It also means that your elbows are separating through impact. Although your hands are holding the rope, if you can get the feel that you're actually pulling it through impact position with your arms, your swing should reflect the correct inside-out swing.

Horizontal to Horizontal

This drill will feel very awkward, but it helps you get the picture and feel for the proper wrist position. Bring the club to that horizontal and parallel position in the backswing/downswing—the position you began with when using the rope. Properly aligned, the wrist of your left hand, if you're a right-handed golfer, is neither cupped (bent toward your forearm) nor bowed (bent away from your forearm), but continues a straight line with the forearm.

As the club moves to and through impact on the way to the finish, it passes through another position: horizontal to the ground and parallel to the target line with your hands once again approximately hip high. When the club passes through this position, that front wrist should still be in a straight line with the forearm.

The drill is simple. Bring the club back to horizontal/parallel, hit the ball, and stop the finish at horizontal/parallel. Check the wrist position. Practice until that flat wrist position happens naturally at both points.

Drill to Increase Club-Head Speed

There are certainly plenty of drills for every facet of the golf swing, but for increasing club-head speed, you need to learn but one. It increases club-head speed in two ways. First and most obviously, it increases the strength of the muscles involved in the swing. Second and often overlooked, it increases flexibility around the fixed axis.

Ready? Get an old worn-out broom and swing it. Okay, there's a bit more to it than that, although not much more. Put a mark on the floor (a piece of tape will do nicely) to represent the golf ball. Address the mark and swing.

To better simulate the grip of a golf club, try taping the end of the broom with athletic tape to about the same length as the grip on the club. The more you can hold the broomstick like a club, the better you can simulate an actual swing, and the more effective the drill.

To swing the broomstick properly, and to avoid pulling a muscle, it's best to start out slowly, perhaps swinging the broomstick as few as ten times a day. You want to eventually work up to 100 swings a day. They don't need to be all at once; you can divide the work load into four sessions. Besides, you don't want fatigue from swinging this stick to create bad habits in your golf swing.

Every swing should be a focused effort on proper takeaway, backswing, downswing, impact, follow-through, and finish. It becomes as much an exercise for the mind as for the body. Don't get careless, do it right.

If you live in an area where winter prevents playing golf, do this drill as an off-season drill. Or, you can use it year round, on days when you aren't out on the course or the practice tee.

Putt Work

Putting is your score saver, and here are some drills guaranteed to make you a better putter. Most people practice putting only before a round of golf, only for a few minutes, and only to build confidence for the upcoming round. That's not bad as far as it goes, but it isn't putt practice.

A House-Bound Drill

You'll be hard-pressed to find a greenskeeper who would permit this drill on the golf course, so practice this one on the carpet at home. You'll need a table with a broad edge high enough to meet your hands at the elevation at which your hands grip the putter. If you have no luck with a table of the right height, often turning a table on its side will do the trick. Align the edge of the table with the line of the straight putt. Practice putting with your hands sliding down the straight line of the table edge. This exercise trains you to hold the line of a putt from the top end.

Length of Putt Stroke

Too many beginners draw back the putter the same distance for putts of every length. They alter the distance the ball rolls by altering the amount of speed they generate in the head of the putter over this one-stroke distance. This drill is designed to help you control the distance of the putt by forcing you to decide how far to draw back the putter.

Start with a flat putt of about six feet and estimate how far back you should draw the head of the putter to roll the ball the desired distance. If you estimate six inches, push a golf tee into the ground eight inches behind the ball, to give your putter its free swing through six inches. Work back on longer putts repeating the same drill, estimating the distance the putter should be drawn back.

FACT

Many weekend golfers never practice. One reason is that they don't know how or what to practice. Another reason is they don't want to. If you practice, you'll get better. If you practice the right way, you'll get better faster.

Two Practice Schedules

If you're having difficulty deciding what to practice and for how long, consider the pair of practice schedules that follow. Each schedule approaches the task from a different perspective. Both schedules will improve your game.

A Practice by the Clock

The advantage of this practice session is that you give roughly equal work to all facets of the game, and neglect none:

1. Begin with the shortest club you carry, hit with a half swing, and increase until full. Then work up from shortest to longest club, hitting each about ten times. **Time elapsed:** One hour.

2. Go directly to the pitching area and practice pitches and pitch and run shots for **twenty-five minutes**.
3. Go to the bunker and practice for **twenty-five minutes**.
4. Practice putting for **twenty-five minutes**.

Total time: Two hours and fifteen minutes.

Practice by Percentage

The advantage of this practice is that you work on your game according to the percentage of shots an average round requires in certain categories. Sixty percent of all golf shots occur within sixty yards of the green. Of that number, 44 percent are putts. Twenty-five percent of all shots are drives from the tee. Armed with that knowledge, here's how you practice by percentage.

Warm up with a short club, then begin. Practice 16 percent of your shots within sixty yards but off the green. Spend 44 percent of your time putting. Spend 25 percent driving. The other 15 percent (and this is key to the percentage practice) is comprised of those types of shots that were weakest on your previous round of golf.

Both of these plans will get results. Try the second plan immediately after a round of golf once you're conditioned enough to maintain your swing and your stamina for that long.

Chapter 19

E Staying in Shape for Golf

To make the most of your golfing experiences, keep your body in good condition. Strength training, stretching, and building up your stamina will help to ward off aches and pains, pulled muscles, and fatigue, while helping you improve your game. This chapter offers exercises and stretches you can do at home to get, or keep, your body in shape.

Strength Training for the Upper Body

Resistance training (weights) have revolutionized sport preparation over the last thirty-five years. There was a time when the common consensus was that certain sports, basketball and golf included, didn't require weight training. In fact, weight training was thought to be hurtful to the pursuit of excellence in the game. Not anymore. Muscular strength and stamina are essential to all sports.

The division of the weight training between upper and lower halves of the body is for convenience only. A chart at the end of the chapter will provide a couple of sample strength programs. Never neglect one half of the body for the other, or even one part of the body for another, unless injury or disability so dictates. All the muscles of the body are important and will respond to exercise, regardless of age.

FACT

Women shouldn't worry about "bulking" up. You couldn't possibly pump enough iron to look brutish, only toned and more beautiful. Besides, resistance training will increase bone density and reduce the risk of osteoporosis.

Strength Training for the Back

Anyone who has ever had back problems can vouch for the prime importance of a sound back. The latissimus dorsi (that large muscle group on either side of the spine and running up the side of the back causing the back to flare in a V shape from the waist) is the largest muscle group in the upper body. Your local YMCA or health club offers several ways to strengthen the "lats"—lat pull downs, bent rows, and cable rows, for example—but you don't need the equipment from a health club to do the job effectively. Good, old-fashioned pull-ups and chin-ups are excellent.

Hang from the monkey bars at the local playground with your palms facing toward your face and pull yourself up until your chin nears or raises above the bar. For a more difficult version of the exercise, turn palms away and pull up. With palms facing toward you, the biceps muscles of your arms assist in the pull. With palms facing away, you rely more on the latissimus dorsi to complete the lift.

Rare is the person who, lacking strength training, can hang from a bar and pull up more than one to three times. Many people can't even pull up once. So, consider beginning with a modified version of the exercise. Grab a bar, suspended only about four feet to five feet off the ground, and extend your legs out in front of you so that your arms are hanging straight down and your feet are still touching the ground. Then pull yourself up from this position. Someone just beginning an exercise program should begin with palms facing, not turned away from the body. This modified version of the pull-up/chin-up reduces the amount of weight your arms and back must lift.

A second exercise focuses on the lower back, the spinal erectus muscles. These are the muscles in the small of your back, the ones most prone to aches after lifting something you wish you hadn't. Stand erect, interlock your fingers, and place your hands behind your head with elbows flared to the sides. (Imagine yourself stretched out in the hammock after mowing the yard in that "ahhh" position with the hands.) Now unlock your knees and bend at the waist until your upper body is parallel to the floor. From this position move slowly and smoothly until you are standing straight again. To make this movement slightly more difficult, stop just short of standing straight, keeping a small amount of tension continuously on your lower back, and hold for a few seconds.

ALERT!

Before beginning any exercise program, it is always best to consult your doctor. Who knows? Your doctor may even be able to advise you on other exercises to help you get in good golfing shape.

Exercises for the Chest

Push-ups are an effective exercise for the muscles of the chest (and arms, for that matter). Best of all, you don't need any equipment for this exercise. Place your hands shoulder-width apart on the floor and extend your body out behind forming a flat surface sloping toward the floor from the back of the head down to the tops of your heels. Lower your body to the floor keeping your back straight, and push up again.

If you can't accomplish several push-ups in a row, try the modified version. This is the same push-up just described, only let your knees rest on the ground rather than trying to stretch out all the way to your feet.

This exercise will also strengthen your shoulders (deltoids), biceps, and triceps.

A Strength Exercise for Your Shoulders

This exercise allows for some creativity. Stand erect with knees unlocked or sit on a bench. Extend your arms straight up toward the ceiling. Now bend your elbows and allow your hands to drop near shoulder height. Then extend your arms straight over your head once more. This exercise is called a military press, or shoulder press. Here's the creativity part. To add resistance, place an unopened can of food in each hand. If you can do three sets of ten easily, you need to add more weight. For more weight, you could use milk jugs half or completely filled with sand or water. Better still, you could use a pair of dumbbells to which weight can be added. The military press will also strengthen your arms.

Exercises for Your Arms

If you do only two exercises for your upper body, do chin-ups and push-ups, since both of these exercises also stimulate the muscles in your arms. For more complete workouts, add biceps curls and a triceps exercise.

With arms hanging straight down at your sides, and some weight gripped in each hand with palms facing the front, curl your arm, raising your fist toward your shoulder and returning it to the starting position. Take care not to rock backward, arching your back to lift the weight. That kind of "cheating" motion keeps your arms from bearing the strain of the exercise and places the wrong kind of stress on your back.

There are many exercises for your triceps. With your push-ups, for instance, you can simply move your hands closer together than shoulder width. The closer your hands are together, the more the movement will emphasize the backs of your arms. Or, using about the same weight that you use for curls, extend your weighted hands straight up toward the ceiling, then one at a time or together, bend your straight arms at the elbow, allowing the weight to drop behind your head, and press straight back toward the ceiling again.

FACT

If you have access to weight equipment you will discover a variety of movements for the triceps as well as for the rest of your upper back, but the exercises mentioned here will suffice for either a beginner or for someone who has done no strength training for a number of years.

Wrist Curls

Wrist curls will strengthen the forearms, but then so will all of the other exercises for the upper body, because they require the hands to grip. Still, if you want to add another exercise, the following will help improve the grip strength and also the stamina of your forearms. That means that the comfortable, sure grip you began the round of golf with will still be comfortable and sure at the end of the round.

Wrist curls are most easily done with light dumbbells, but your imagination can guide you. Sit so that the tops of your thighs are roughly parallel to the floor. Rest your forearms on your thighs so that your hands are angled in front of your knees from the wrists. Slowly lower your hand so that a dumbbell gradually rolls down the length of your palm and into your fingers, then raise your hand as high as it will go. Repeat the set with the other hand.

Strength Training for the Lower Body

Your local YMCA or health club has fitness equipment allowing you to select from a variety of exercises to train your legs. But you don't need access to a weight room to develop a good regime for making your legs more powerful and increasing your stamina.

An Exercise for the Thighs and Glutes

The squat is the best overall exercise for the legs. The squat strengthens the quadriceps muscles in the front of the thigh, the hamstring (or biceps femoris) in the back of the thigh, and the gluteus maximus, that large muscle mass comprising your buttocks.

The best type of squat for a beginner is called the "box" squat. It's best performed when straddling a bench, but it can be done using a small chair with a narrow seat. Straddle the bench, legs comfortably apart. Keeping your feet fully on the floor, lower your body until your buttocks touch the bench, without bounding off of the bench or resting in a seated position. Then push with your legs to return to a standing position. To increase the intensity of the exercise, use a lower bench and never return to a full standing position, but stop just short, maintaining constant tension on your legs.

Calf Raises to Complete the Routine

Stand so that the weight of your body is supported by the balls of your feet resting on the edge of a step. Lower your heels as far as they will drop below the level of the step; pause for a second, then push up until you're standing with your heels high in the air; hold for another second, and repeat. The intensity of this exercise may be increased by holding a small weight in one hand and using the other for balance, or simply by standing on one foot instead of two.

ALERT!

You aren't superman, so don't try to be. Start out slow and work your way up to higher intensity strength training. You will feel the stretch and exertion of the muscles, but if you feel pain while doing any of these exercises, stop what you're doing and consult your doctor.

Strengthening the Abdominals

While no area of the body ought to be neglected by the beginning golfer—or any adult concerned about preserving health—the muscles of the abdominal region are often ignored. But the abdominals do much more for the human body (and for the golfer) than help to hold in the belly. The abdominals provide stability to the spine and to the torso. More important, strong abdominals reduce strain in the spine and help prevent lower back problems.

Swinging the golf club will do an adequate job of strengthening the obliques (the muscles of the midsection located more toward the sides of the body), but certain specific exercises are best for improving the strength of the main abdominal muscle group: the rectus abdominus— that "six-pack" above and below your belly button.

Crunches

If you haven't exercised for a while, crunches are a great way to begin. Lay flat on the floor with your knees bent and back flat. Cross your hands over your chest and lift your shoulders and shoulder blades off the floor. Exhale as you contract your abdominals and hold the contraction for a second, then ease back to the floor. Don't rest. Immediately repeat the movement and continue to do it as long as you can comfortably, making certain you're lifting your shoulder blades clear of the floor each time.

Once that crunch becomes easy, begin in the same position, but now try keeping continuous tension on your abdominals. The difference in this more intense movement is that you never allow your shoulders to return to the floor.

Advanced Crunches

Begin in the same basic crunch position. Now raise your legs so that the fronts of your thighs are perpendicular to the floor. Interlace your fingers and place your hands behind your head. As you lift your shoulders from the floor, twist your torso so that your right elbow rotates toward your left knee, and draw your left knee toward your right elbow at the same time. Return your left leg to the perpendicular position and your right elbow to its starting position. Repeat with left elbow and right leg. Shooting for several sets of this movement with fifteen to twenty repetitions per set is a good beginner's target.

Bent Knee Sit-Ups

Begin with your back flat on the floor, with knees bent and your feet flat on the floor. You may wish to do this exercise with your feet tucked under a heavy object, or have someone hold you by the ankles. With arms crossed over your chest, raise your torso off of the ground and toward your knees. Then lower your torso back toward the floor. This exercise will also strengthen hip flexors, a small muscle in the upper thigh.

ALERT!

Avoid doing sit-ups with legs stretched straight out. While many people have no problem at all, those who haven't maintained an exercise program over the years, or those who have had back problems, may find that this type of sit-up increases back problems.

Switch around among these abdominal exercises when you become bored. Or, look for books containing a variety of exercises to keep your workouts fresh.

Stretches to Improve the Swing Motion

Most adults who sit in an office most of the day are stiff. Even if you have found time to swing a club every day of your life from the time you could walk, you're most likely not as limber as you once were. The older you get, the more effort you must make to maintain flexibility. Even if you're already stiff as old leather, you can recover much of the youthful suppleness. Stretching will not only help your golf swing, it will improve your quality of life.

Do these stretches every morning when you first get up. Do them right. Hold each stretch for twenty seconds. For each of them, turn, twist, or bend until you feel the intended muscle group, but keep the "stretch" comfortable. If the stretch is painful, you're pushing, pulling, or twisting too hard and tempting injury. Are you in a hurry for results? Then do them three times a day. You will be stunned at your rapid improvement.

To do this entire regimen correctly takes about seven minutes. Add an extra layer of physical protection to your golf game and do these stretches just before you walk out onto the course and swing your first club of the day. It will be the other members of your foursome who complain about pulling necks, backs, and calf muscles, not you.

The Neck Stretch

Stand comfortably with good posture and feet about shoulder width apart. With shoulders square, turn your head to the left and look over your shoulder. With the fingers of your right hand, press against your right jaw or right side of your face to accentuate the head turn. Press gently and maintain a comfortable stretching sensation for twenty seconds. Turn your head to the right and repeat the process with the fingers of your left hand pressing on the left side of your face.

For the Muscles of the Rotator Cuff

Do both of the following two stretches. Extend your right arm straight out in front of you and parallel to the floor. Bend your right arm at the elbow, bringing the right forearm across your body to the left, still parallel to the floor. With your left hand, grab your right elbow from underneath and pull your right elbow toward the left until you achieve a comfortable stretch. Hold for the twenty count. Switch sides. Remember to keep your shoulders and hips as square as you can.

QUESTION?

What is the rotator cuff?
The rotator cuff is an intricate symphony of muscles that combine to move the whole upper quadrant of your back that supports the shoulder. Raise your arm and throw a ball; you're using the rotator cuff. Swim, and you are using the rotator cuff to pull yourself through the water. Grab a golf club and swing; again, you're using the rotator cuff.

For the second stretch, extend your right arm straight up over your head. Bend your arm at the elbow, allowing the right forearm to fall naturally behind your head. With your left hand, reach behind your head and grab the right elbow. Pull, holding a comfortable stretch, for twenty seconds. Then repeat with the other side.

Lateral Stretch

With the same comfortable square stance, place your right hand on your right hip. Press against your right hip, pushing it toward the left. You will feel a stretch in two places: up and down the outside of your left leg (and maybe left side of your torso), and on the inner side of your right leg. After twenty seconds, place your left hand on the left hip and push.

Stretching the Back (and the Chest)

Drop to the floor and stretch out face down. Position your hands beside your shoulders. Press up as if to do a push-up, but raise only your torso off the floor, keeping your legs and hips flat on the ground. With your back arched hold the comfortable stretch for the usual time.

If you're really stiff, you may find that you can't start from the floor (the preferred way) and push up with your arms; you can only lift yourself a short distance and your arms tire before the stretch can be completed. If so, then try this. Start from a push-up position: arms shoulder width apart and extended toward the floor directly below the shoulders, palms flat on the floor, and on your toes, with the neck, back, and legs in straight alignment. Gently sag from the hips, keeping your arms straight, while trying to use the arch of your back to ease the lower half of your body toward the floor.

Be gentle. Go slow. Do this every day, and you will improve quickly.

Modified Hurdler's Stretch

Stay down on the floor, but sit up. Stretch out your right leg in front of you. Bend your left leg so that your left foot touches the inside surface of your right leg somewhere between your right knee and right groin. Stop right there. If you're quite stiff, this position alone may be an accomplishment. If you already feel a stretch sitting like this, and if to continue with the following description creates discomfort, let this position be your stretch, until it "feels" too easy. Then proceed as follows.

Bend from the waist and reach for your right toe with both hands. You will likely feel a stretch in your right hamstring, in your back, your groin, and your waist. Hold the stretch. Then repeat with the other side. With this stretch, you'll easily note your progress as your hands slowly creep down your leg, maybe even past your toes.

ALERT!

Don't overdo it. Listen to your body. How can you tell if you're working the stretch too vigorously? If your breathing is strained and coming in gasps, you're pushing far too fast.

Standing Wall Stretch

You may have seen runners do this one. It looks as if they're holding up a wall or telephone pole. Stand about arm's length from the wall. With your palms flat against the wall, lean in toward the wall. Put one foot in front of your body, and the other behind your body. Keep the front foot flat and press the heel of the back foot down to stretch. You'll feel the stretch from your heel all the way up your calf muscle. Don't overdo it, especially if you're trying to undo decades of sedentary living. A torn muscle, or worse, a torn tendon, will set you back several months. Then change feet and repeat the stretch.

A variation of this exercise that allows for a greater intensity of the stretch—once you've worked up to it—is to place the foot of the leg you are not stretching forward, within a few inches of the wall. This will allow you to flex at the waist and further stretch the other calf. Hold a comfortable stretch and don't bounce.

Side Stretch

Now turn so that your shoulders are perpendicular to the wall. You can adjust your distance from the wall according to the amount of stretch your body can handle. With the hand closest to the wall, reach up as high as possible and place your palm flat against its surface. Assuming your left hand is against the wall, push your right hip, the outside hip, toward the wall and hold the stretch. Feel will vary a bit, but you're likely to feel this stretch in your hips, back, along the side of the body closest to the wall, and in your abdominals. Hold for twenty seconds and repeat with the other side.

FACT

To stretch your chest, stand before an open doorway and place a hand on either side of the doorjam. Lean in until you feel the stretch across your chest, and hold it for twenty seconds.

Stretches for Warm-Up

Assuming you're committed to keeping your body in good condition by following an exercise regimen, warm-up before a round of golf should be a snap. Run through the seven-minute stretching program we've just explained. That's best. If you're extremely pinched for time, then stretch the calves as described, use the modified hurdler's stretch for the hamstrings, do a few squats to cover the front of the thighs and your glutes, and save your torso for the first tee.

At the tee, grab a club out of your bag and place it across your shoulders. With legs about shoulder width apart, begin a gentle rotating motion side to side, with back straight and head straight ahead. When your body no longer feels tight, tilt over side to side, letting the left shoulder tip toward the left foot. Return to the upright position and tilt the right shoulder toward right foot, and return to upright again.

Then grip the club as you would to hit the ball and swing the club in an easy motion—backswing to follow-through to backswing to follow-through, and so on. Swing easy, stretching a bit further than normal at the both ends of the swing. This motion will also get your shoulders and arms, and to a lesser degree, your chest, prepared for battle on the links.

Sample Exercise Programs

Any exercise program should have at least these two objectives: work every part of the body and be doable—not so daunting as to discourage regular training. The following training programs are designed with those two goals in mind.

Two Days per Week Option (Monday and Thursday)

If you're not stretching every morning, at least stretch before strength training. And, if you're stretching once a day, stretching again before strength training will serve as a warm-up and also increase your flexibility much, much quicker.

Two Days per Week Program	
Exercise	**Number of Sets and Repetitions**
Squats	Work up to 3 sets of 15 (3 × 15)
Modified chin-ups/ pull-ups	Up to 3 × 15 (once achieved, try one set of regular chin-/pull-ups and finish with 2 × 15 modified)
Push-ups	Up to 3 × 20, then set goal of 1 × 50
Military press	Up to 3 × 15, then add more weight
Crunches	Up to 3 × 20
Biceps curls	Up to 3 × 15
Triceps curls	Up to 3 × 15
Calf raises	Up to 3 × 15, then add weight or switch to one-legged calf raises

Begin with only one set per exercise. Once the top number of repetitions is achieved, add a second set, then a third. Rest one minute between each set. Including stretches, this simple program with three sets per exercise should take about thirty minutes.

Four Days per Week Program

Again, be sure to stretch before beginning to exercise.

Four Days per Week Program	
Monday and Thursday	**Tuesday and Friday**
Squats	Chin-ups/pull-ups
Crunches	Push-ups
Calf raises	Military press
	Crunches
	Biceps curls
	Triceps curls

There are many good fitness books on the market, so don't let boredom stop you from your physical training regime. Adding variety to your workout will yield greater results and make for less tedious workouts. Ⓔ

Chapter 20

Golf for Everyone

No one is too old or too young to take up the game. Anyone who can grip a club, regardless of his or her particular physical challenges, can learn to play and to play successfully. You can compete against yourself, the course, and other players.

Maximizing a Single Trip to the Range

The key to maximizing a trip to the practice range is having a plan. If you're new to the game, it's probably best to write your plan down. Make a covenant with yourself that you'll stick by your plan, and that you'll evaluate your plan only after you've finished at the range.

Before you swing a club, summon to mind the three imperatives: swing around a fixed axis, keep the front wrist flat, and swing in path. Say them to yourself or write them down on your plan sheet. Put them in your mind, and, over time, they will become ingrained in your game.

The Basics

Three things belong in any trip to the range for purposes other than just warming up for a round: stretching, hitting ten to fifteen balls per club, and hitting 100 putts.

Do your stretches every day and stretch again just before going to the range, or stretch at the range. Let other people be the ones who complain about getting the sore neck or sore back from golf. Then work through your bag of clubs. Some people go right for the driver. Don't. Start out with the wedges and work toward the longer-shafted clubs. Or, consider beginning with one of the middle irons, a five, six, or seven. Those clubs tend to be the clubs that are easiest to swing correctly. From that point on, you can vary the club selection a bit.

Hit the ten balls with the five iron, for example, then hit a short iron, a nine, or a wedge, then a long iron. Repeat the cycle with another middle iron, then a short iron, and this time perhaps the three wood: middle, short, long, middle, short, long. Eventually, you will find a cycle that fits you and that gives you the most confidence. You may find the wedge, nine, and so on, up to the driver, works best for you. Regardless, be methodical and patient with yourself.

Be target conscious. Always aim at something on the range—the flags, or the yardage signs. This habit will improve your accuracy and boost your confidence in distance control.

Hitting Putts

After hitting with every club, hit a hundred putts. You can use some of the putting drills, or save those drills for sessions in which you work on putts only. Vary the lengths of your putts and work on reading the putts accurately.

Pick three distances to feature in the putt practice portion of the session. Try four-foot putts (those will make three-foot putts look so easy), eight-foot putts (sometimes your lags and pitches are not so great), and twenty-foot putts (no one wants to three putt from that close). Your rationale will change from time to time regarding the distances to feature. Here's another set: three-foot putts (they are must-makes), five-foot putts (the par savers), and fifteen-foot putts (a typical birdie length putt).

ALERT!

Some studies indicate that the most effective stretching occurs after the muscles have exercised and are still warm. Consider increasing the benefits of stretches by spending seven minutes before and after exercise to keep the kinks out and help develop your flexibility faster.

Extra Help for the Trip to the Range

Sixty percent of shots occur within 100 yards of the hole. Save some balls to pitch and to pitch and run. Take aim at the range flags, or if those targets are too far, identify something on the ground closer. Play some of these shorter shots to hit your target and then roll. Play others to run to your target.

Take a video camera and tape a few swings from directly behind and, with the camera facing you, from the opposite side of the ball from your stance. Later, at home, this footage will can help you diagnose your swing, help you make corrections, or help reinforce your developing confidence in your golf swing.

Selecting Your Most Reliable Clubs

Insert this thought into your brain about reliable clubs and let it work for you: Master the basic swing motion and every club in your bag should be reliable. You hit the driver with the same motion as you hit the wedge, the seven wood, a one iron, a six iron, and so on. Every club is designed to be used for certain situations that a golfer will encounter over a round or two of golf. Some day you'll probably come upon a situation where you'll use every stick in the bag in thirty-six, if not eighteen, holes. Learn to use them all.

Be Confident with Your Clubs and Swing

Every golfer has certain clubs in which he or she has greater confidence. For example, some golfers always go for the green, even those surrounded by traps, because they hit sand shots as well as most golfers hit lag putts. Some golfers plan for approach shots to be hit from certain distances because a particular club in the bag gives them superior distance control over another club, or at least they believe it does. This can be particularly true for a course with frequent gusty winds; many golfers learn to count on longer irons flying beneath the wind.

In a perfect world, you would hit all clubs equally well. That should be your goal if you plan to improve your game past a certain high-handicap range. The reality is every golfer finds certain clubs he or she has more confidence in. Over the years those clubs may change. Still, master them all and your scoring will improve.

Regardless which clubs are your favorites, consider adding the driver and the putter to your list, because they are the clubs that help you score.

The Physical Reason

The swing mechanics of a beginner, no matter how studied and practiced, won't be as efficient as the swing of a good golfer. It will take months and years to develop a terrific swing. If you do become a student of the game, your swing may continue to improve over a couple of decades, which means you'll learn to generate more club-head speed with less effort.

Then the day will come when it dawns on you that you're hitting certain clubs in your bag better than you're hitting others. You may even decide that you've regressed as a golfer. The probable cause of your loss of confidence is that *you* have changed but your clubs haven't. It may be as simple a problem as changing grips on your clubs. They may have gotten slick or worn. You may be gripping the clubs harder than you should be gripping them, reducing the club-head speed and throwing your swing timing off just enough to make the club unreliable.

An even more likely culprit is that, as your swing improves, you may find the flex of the shafts on your current clubs makes control more of a problem. You're likely to discover that the longer clubs are the ones you're losing the most control over. Or, if you've always loved hitting a full wedge, it may gradually become much less accurate.

The bottom line is if you can generate great club-head speed, you may need a less flexible shaft. If age or illness has reduced your ability to deliver that speed to the ball, you may require a more flexible shaft.

FACT

Even the pros develop flaws in their swings from time to time. If something goes awry, make an appointment with a pro and let the pro watch you. If the pro suggests a change in shafts, experiment. It just might be the quickest path to improving your game.

Selecting a Driver and a Putter

There's more variation among drivers and putters on the market than for any other club. That's because golfers instinctively know that these clubs are the scoring clubs. Excellent drives, confident drives, set up the approach shots. Putts save strokes. Quite often, a good golfer will have a putter and driver that seem out of place with the rest of the matched set of clubs from three iron through three wood. That's because the golfer has confidence in those two particular clubs.

The normal driver is forty-four to forty-five inches long. But some people prefer drivers fifty inches long. The loft on a standard driver is about twelve degrees, but some golfers prefer drivers with less loft. Some prefer whippier shafts on their drivers than on other clubs, but if you swing hard already, a whippy shaft on the driver could lead to trouble.

Esthetics are important with a driver. If it looks good to you and feels good, you'll probably hit it well. If it feels like a farmer's maul, like something made for driving fence posts, it's probably not right for you. You want it to feel fast in your hands, and to look fast to your eyes.

With the putter, esthetics are also important. Crazy as it seems, the club must look to you as if it will improve your accuracy and touch, and it must feel that way, too. Putter shafts vary in length. And believe it or not, loft on the face of the putter varies, too.

ESSENTIAL

There's not a lot to be said about changing putters. But, if you've lost your touch, though your putting drills are flawless, borrow another putter or buy a new one. Odds are, your putting will improve, at least for a while.

Business Golf

Fact of life: Business decisions are made on the golf course; it's no secret that deals are made and people are hired during many a round of golf.

Assessing the Character and Closing a Deal

Many companies feel that the measure of a candidate or prospective business partner can be taken in a round of golf. How honest is the person? Does that person fudge when marking the ball on the green? Take liberties when dropping the ball? Is the person competitive, yet appreciative of an opponent's quality play? You'll learn a person's communications skills and command of the language, and get to access personality traits and sense of humor when playing golf. A round of golf can bring out a person's civility, sportsmanship, competitive fire, and even integrity.

It isn't a matter of how well a potential business partner or president plays the game. What's important is the conversation between shots, the way the candidate handles a shanked shot that races into the water, how complimentary the person is of another's good efforts, how the candidate controls his or her temper, welcomes competition, celebrates victory, and handles defeat. This type of talk about the royal and ancient game may seem hokey and sentimental to the uninitiated, but it's a fact of life.

FACT

Some corporations hire professional golfers (teaching pros usually) to take clients on golf outings. There the clients get to enjoy the game in the company of fine golfers—everyone loves watching good golf up close. The pros also give tips. Clients often can't wait until business brings them back for more.

Handling the Business Golf Invitation

So, what does a beginner do if confronted with a business golf invitation? If you've never picked up a club in your life, say so. The invitation may be withdrawn, or pushed on you. In either case, get thee to a practice range, preferably under the tutelage of a pro, and learn the fundamentals.

When you first play business golf, play to your ability and know your limitations. If you've got to hit three irons off the tee to keep the ball playable, do it. Play wisely as your ability dictates; that will be a significant plus in your favor to observant eyes.

Starting Junior Off Right

Every parent or grandparent who plays the game wants to pass on the tradition to the younger generation. Golf is one of the few lifetime sports. The family may dream of Junior growing up to become the next Nancy Lopez, Betsy King, Arnold Palmer, or Tiger Woods, but deep down they'll be just as happy if the child develops a love of the game that can be shared and played among the generations. Is there any other game in which four generations can compete against each other in the same foursome?

It's important for a young child to know that golf is play and something to have fun with. A youngster can comprehend golf as play only for as long as he or she is happy doing it. Before the fussing starts, it's time to quit.

Helping your child to develop as a golfer requires you to use your creativity and patience, as well as your instincts about family bonding and play. Bank your competitive fires. Stifle the parental desire to live vicariously through your daughter's or son's accomplishments or to satisfy your ego with his or her textbook swing. The suggestions that follow are based upon the successful rearing of a real child into a ranked golfer, a typical child in all respects from the get go.

Take Junior to the Range

Mom and Dad love the game, so before Junior can walk, one or the other occasionally takes Junior to the range, parking him or her in one of those kiddie seats on rollers so Junior can tiptoe around. The nice thing about those rollers on the bottom is that they don't roll on grass, so Junior can never creep too close and get a face full of golf club.

When Junior gets tired, Mom and Dad quit. It is that simple. Parents' priorities change. Dad's silky smooth swing is no longer quite so important (and won't be for about eighteen years).

Take great care choosing a teacher for a young child—if you decide to go that route at all. Almost every teacher knows all the right stuff, but not every teacher can share knowledge with a five-year-old.

Once Junior can toddle, the child receives a gift of an oversized plastic golf club and a big plastic golf ball. Then Junior and Mom or

Dad go to the range together. The parent doesn't get to hit a lot of balls, and is always careful to go to the range when it's most likely vacant. When Mom takes Junior she finds a spot where Junior is always in view but out of the way of other golfers. As she hits a ball, Junior hits the big plastic ball with the big plastic golf club. After five minutes, Junior is ready to chase butterflies. Mom sneaks a few more shots and calls it quits. Dad performs the same routine when it's his turn to take Junior to the range.

The First Club and (Maybe) First Lesson

Junior's a big kid now, four or five years old. For Junior's birthday, this big kid gets a real club, a cut-down seven wood. The local pro has the knowledge to determine, based on size of the child, what types of clubs are light enough and the proper length. Dad hits a ball, Junior watches. Junior hits a ball, Dad watches. On it goes back and forth. After five to ten minutes, the butterflies have Junior's interest again. Quittin' time.

Don't rush to correct swing flaws. Flaws are not flaws to a child; they're part of play. Let the kid play. Most children aren't interested enough at an early age to pay attention to a correction; in fact, most will rebel against it. Then where will you be? Get angry or frustrated, and it is no longer play.

Junior swings the club cross-handed. Friends who know the high caliber of Mom and Dad's respective games are petrified. They rush to call Dad's attention to the horrid swing mechanics. They're more horrified to learn that Mom and Dad don't care. (What kind of parents are these?!) Dad says of Junior: "The kid'll change the grip when the kid's ready to change it."

A Round of Golf Together

Mom and Dad hit from the tee, then Junior hits from the shortest tee. They walk to Junior's twenty-yard shot and pick up the ball. Junior gets to play the second shot from the spot where Dad's ball landed. Junior gets tired after nine holes. They all quit.

The club pro sees what's going on out on the course, and the pro likes it. Mom and Dad are teaching Junior without slowing up play. Junior doesn't play three hundred little shots; Junior plays only from Dad's spot.

FACT

Young children develop at different rates. Just because your neighbor's eight-year-old drives the ball 230 yards and looks like he trains on Muscle Beach, doesn't mean your child, who sometimes spins all the way around when swinging the club, won't be U.S. Amateur Champ in ten short years.

A Tourney-Tested Veteran

Junior, age eight, has learned enough about the game to enter a tournament. The tees are shorter because all the other junior players are just learning the game, too. Just like kids on the baseball diamond, some of the older ones already know a lot about the rules, and they're quick to convey what they know to younger violators. Kids teach other kids well. Then Junior takes that knowledge back to the range with Dad. At the tournament, Junior noticed how well some of the other kids hit the ball, and now Junior watches Dad hit it far and straight. Without a word, Junior uncrosses the old grip and begins making adjustments. Dad offers a suggestion.

Junior Wants More

Junior realizes that what Dad does at the range is called practice, and that once in awhile, Mom or Dad takes a lesson. Junior connects taking a lesson with playing better, and wants lessons, too. Give Junior what Junior can handle, but remember the old showbiz adage, "Leave 'em wanting more."

Mom and Dad find their own way to say how important it is to learn and to practice if you want to do anything well, even golf. The end result? An outstanding Junior golfer.

Distances Are Different for Women

There is absolutely no difference in the rules for golf for men and women. It's the same game. However, men do hit the ball farther than women so there are differing yardages for the women's game—the yardages are shorter.

Difference in Yardage

Generally, the teeing areas for women are in front of the teeing areas for men. There may be occasional holes on a few golf courses where one of the men's teeing areas is within a few yards of one of the women's teeing areas, but that is an exception. The rules of golf do not require the yardage differences, but there are recommended yardages for USGA tournaments. The yardage from women's tees for most golf courses ranges from about 6,000 yards to about 6,200 yards. The yardage for most men's tees ranges from 6,600 to 7,000 yards. It isn't as though these differences are random; keep in mind the game has been evolving for six hundred years.

FACT

Just as handicaps are used to even the playing field for differing abilities, the differences in yardage for men and women are meant to keep the game competitively fair among all players. It's certainly not meant to be biased toward one sex or the other.

LPGA versus PGA

The intent of the differences in teeing areas is ingenious really, and can best be seen in those tour challenges in which a member of the LPGA competes against a member of the PGA and the men's Senior PGA. Each member of such a threesome will tee off from a separate teeing area. The PGA golfer from the teeing area farthest back from the green is followed by the Senior PGA golfer driving from a teeing area not so far back, who is followed by the LPGA golfer from a teeing area closer to the green.

After all three have teed off, the PGA member is apt to be 150 yards from the flag, the Senior PGA golfer 140 yards away, and the LPGA player 125 yards from the pin. For each of those three players, the distance from ball to flag is roughly an eight iron.

See the genius? They're equal in what club they need off the tee, and equal on the club required for approach to the green. Women beginners are at no disadvantage.

Playing as a Senior

After retiring, it is common for men and women to take up a hobby or activity to fill the void left when leaving a career. Often, golf worms its way into the hearts of seniors for this very reason. Some seniors take up the game to remain physically active and have fun at the same time. Golf is also a great social activity that can bring together family and friends. Regardless of your reasons for taking up the game, golf offers physical and mental challenges that seniors are never too old to take advantage of.

The seniors who get a decent game going quickest are the ones who've been athletes over the years, who've kept their juices going and their bodies supple with exercise. The senior golfers who have never been athletically inclined are the ones who tend to have the most difficulty developing a golf game, at least at first. The reason for this difference is fitness: muscular strength and stamina, and perhaps most importantly, flexibility.

ALERT!

Don't let ego get in the way of your golf as you age. When the day comes that you need to take out a longer club for each shot, take it. If a course has senior tees, use them. The challenges of golf are still there. Golf's rules intend to allow everyone to compete no matter their age.

Start off slow and learn to improve your game. You'll probably want to develop a regular stretching routine, and perhaps even add some strength training. It's important to stay active and physically fit, not only to improve your golf game, but also to prevent injury. You know best your limitations and/or areas in which you need to improve. Just don't overdo it. Let your game develop slowly and smoothly. Even if you and your retirement buddies are just looking for fun, don't underestimate the physical aspects of the game. Ⓔ

Appendices

Appendix A
Resources

Appendix B
Glossary

Appendix A

Resources

Books about Golf

Very fine books filled with great tips frequently hit the market. Some of those featured in the following list are classics, foundational works that have withstood the test of time. Others are simply great books that any golfer, beginner or experienced, will find helpful.

▶ Cochran, A. J. *The Search for the Perfect Swing*. Philadelphia: Lippincott, 1968.

One of the earliest books of pure research on the golf swing. A team of physiologists and scientists were assembled to analyze the swings of the top pros and determine what makes a swing work. If you like physics, you'll like this book.

▶ Greene, Susan. *The ABC's of Golf*. Dearborn, Mich.: Excel Pub., 1996.

Here's a great way for parents to introduce their children to golf and teach them the ABC's at the same time. The book is filled with playful illustrations of golf clubs, golf balls, tees, and golf shoes, with educational rhymes to go with them.

▶ Harmon, Claude, and John Andrisani. *The Four Cornerstones of Winning Golf*. New York: Simon & Schuster, 1996.

From the "hottest instructor in golf" learn the same secrets Harmon learned from his legendary instructor-father. Harmon's clients include Greg Norman, Davis Love III, and Tiger Woods. The book covers the swing, the short game, and the mental game, as well as staying in physical shape.

▶ Hogan, Ben. *Five Lessons: The Modern Fundamentals of Golf*. New York: Simon & Schuster, 1985.

This is often considered one of the best books ever written on playing the game of golf. Some members of the PGA Tour carry the book with them on tour. It was originally published as a series in *Sports Illustrated* in the early fifties.

▶ Kelley, Homer. *The Golfing Machine.* Seattle: Star System Press, 1983

This book has gathered quite a following. The book is complex and is demanding on the reader. Some of Kelley's teaching is controversial, but there are many proponents of his methodology among the finest teachers of the game today.

▶ Matthew, Sidney, ed. *Secrets of the Master: The Best of Bobby Jones.* Chelsea, Mich.: Sleeping Bear Press, 1996.

Learn the game from Jones, perhaps the best golfer ever to grace the greens, from his own personal writings of the 1920s and 1930s. Jones discusses his secrets of a good golf swing and how to improve every aspect of your game with humorous anecdotes and refreshingly candid views.

▶ Pelz, Dave. *Putt Like the Pros.* New York: Harper & Row, 1989.

The short-game master gives you scientific ways to improve your putting stroke.

▶ Penick, Harvey. *For All Who Love the Game.* New York: Simon & Schuster, 1995.

This book offers lessons and teachings for women.

▶ Rotella, Robert J. *Golf Is Not a Game of Perfect.* New York: Simon & Schuster, 1995

The bestselling mental guru of golf discusses how to master and enjoy the game.

▶ Whitworth, Kathy, and Rhonda Glenn. *Golf for Women.* New York: St. Martin's Press, 1990.

An enjoyable guide to golf from the woman's point of view.

Golf Videos

As with books, excellent golf videos come out all the time. Below are a few that are noteworthy.

▶ *Beginning Golf for Women.* Essentially two videos covering the long game and the short game. Available separately or together as a unit.

▶ *Ben Hogan in Pursuit of Perfection.* Recently unearthed footage taken by a fan of Hogan perfecting his game; this rare inside view of instruction is fast becoming a collector's item.

▶ *David Leadbetter's Simple Solutions for Great Golf.* Twenty-five quick and simple solutions to assist players at every level.

▶ *How I Played Golf.* In 1931, Bobby Jones made a series of movie shorts that featured cameos from Hollywood stars. The tapes were recently discovered in storage and transferred onto video. As you're watching, remember that Jones didn't have the benefit of today's technology and editing capabilities. He executes perfect shots one right after the other, live.

▶ *Johnny Miller's Golf Tips.* Great tips to help golfers play better.

▶ *Kathy Whitworth's Breaking 100.* Whitworth gives five steps to lower your score. Great for golfers of all abilities. There's also a bonus segment here entitled "How to Practice on a Driving Range."

▶ *Little Green Video.* Penick's second instructional video with Ben Crenshaw and Tom Kite.

▶ *Little Red Video.* Highlights from Penick's *Little Red Book.*

▶ *Moe Norman: Golf's Journey.* Through the use of stop-action and slow motion, you get to see one of the most effective and responsible swings on the planet.

▶ *Nice Shot!* Chuck Hogan steps away from conventional wisdom and breaks down the mental part of game, covering exercises, instruction, and forming good habits. If you're looking for something different and effective, this is it.

▶ *Nick Faldo's Fixes.* Faldo shares long-term solutions for golfers' most common difficulties.

▶ *Nick Faldo's Tips and Drills.* Faldo gives his personally developed regime of drills and practice tips, many of which you can use on a daily basis.

▶ *Ray Floyd's Cutting Strokes.* Ray focuses on the short game with creative secrets on pitching, bunker shots, and putting.

▶ *Sixty Yards In.* Ray Floyd focuses on what clubs to select for the short game, including instruction on sand play and putting.

Golf Magazines

Following are periodicals relating to golf. In some instances, the publisher will send you a free sample of its magazine for you to peruse and decide if you'd like to subscribe. Not included are the numerous regional golf magazines with focus on golf courses within each area's purview.

Golf
▶ Circulation: 1.3 million +
▶ Written for: All golfers
▶ Published: Monthly
▶ Web site: ✑ *www.golfonline.com*
▶ To subscribe: Call ✆ 1-800-876-7726

Like *Golf Digest,* these folks are an entire industry unto themselves and are known in the business as *Golf* Magazine Properties. How involved in the industry are they? Well, for openers, they own the Golf Channel. The layout of this magazine reads like an eighteen-hole course. Each "chapter" is noted with a number resembling a hole. This is actually a good idea, as it helps the reader and the magazine focus on each issue it addresses. For instance, the first hole is called "Within the Rules." Hole four is the "Short Game." Hole fourteen is "Health," and so on. It's very well put together and covers a lot of ground.

Golf Digest

▶ Circulation: 1.5 million +
▶ Written for: Beginning to advanced golfers
▶ Published: Monthly
▶ Web site: ✍ *www.golfdigest.com*
▶ To subscribe: Call ✆ 1-800-PAR-GOLF (727-4653)

This is not only a magazine, but an entire golf industry. The company owns and operates a network of over 375 golf schools across the nation. The instructors at these schools are top professionals and contribute to the instructional part of the magazine. In fact, a whole section every month is devoted to instruction. Departments have names like Mind on Golf, The Advisor, Travel Information Service, and Instant Lesson. Although the magazine's readership is predominantly male, there are special sections devoted to women. More and more women, especially in the business world, are playing golf and *Golf Digest* recognizes this. Profiles of great golfers, as well as top-100 course rankings and top-75 public course rankings are an enjoyable and valuable tool. The magazine is immersed deeply in the golf world and is both dedicated and devoted to it.

Golf Illustrated

▶ Circulation: 250,000 +
▶ Published: Bimonthly
▶ Written for: Amateurs and professionals
▶ Web site: ✍ *www.golfillustrated.com*

▶ To subscribe: Call ✆ 1-800-554-1999

Revamped several years ago, *Golf Illustrated* has one of the longest-running track records in the magazine arena. Sports psychologists contribute their views on the mental side of the game in practically every issue. There's advice here, too, on the best resort and general public-access courses to play. Regular features include articles and tips on fitness, swing mechanics, and saving strokes.

Golf Journal (Published by the USGA)

▶ Circulation: (approx.) 525,000
▶ Written for: All golfers
▶ Published: Nine times a year
▶ Web site: ✎ *www.golfjournal.org*
▶ To subscribe: Free with membership in the USGA.
Call ✆ 1-800-345-USGA.

The *Golf Journal* is very informative without being slick. It features articles on golf-course design, golf clubs, history, new equipment, and the USGA championships. One thing the *Golf Journal* has that many publications don't have is information on handicapping.

Golf Tips

▶ Circulation: (approx.) 275,000
▶ Written for: Beginners, amateurs, and professionals
▶ Published: Monthly, except bimonthly in Jan./Feb., Sept./Oct., and Nov./Dec.
▶ Web site: ✎ *www.golftipsmag.com*
▶ To subscribe: Call ✆ 1-800-283-4640

Known as the "Game's Most In-depth Instruction & Equipment Magazine," *Golf Tips*'s goal is to educate devoted golfers. There are tips on instruction, equipment, and travel. Along with featured articles on instruction, there are the monthly departments, some of which include

"New and Notable," a column that focuses on the latest and greatest equipment and apparel; "Fore Women," thoughts about the game from the woman's perspective; "12 Tips from 12 Pros," a column from America's top teachers offering advice on common swing flaws; and seven more departments. Each issue devotes an in-depth article to a golf school.

Golfweek
▶ Circulation: 75,000
▶ Written for: Amateur and professional devotees
▶ Published: Weekly
▶ Web site: ✍ *www.golfweek.com*
▶ To subscribe: Call ✆ 1-800-996-4653

Do you enjoy the game so much that monthly publications aren't quite enough for you? Luckily, there's *Golfweek*. This magazine is similar to a newspaper, providing up-to-the-minute information on who's playing where, standings, and when new equipment is coming onto the marketplace. A column called "The Forecaddie" gives cutting-edge news about the game. Then there's the weekly behind-the-scenes look at how television covers the game, as well as schedules for upcoming events on television. *Golfweek* covers amateur and international news too, and lists all of the tours' scoreboards. Last but not least, there are pages highlighting business and travel. *Golfweek* is enjoyable and easy to read. And if you want to get into the golf business, *Golfweek* publishes a biweekly industry report for golf retailers and operators.

Golf for Women
▶ Circulation: (approx.) 330,000
▶ Published: Monthly
▶ Written for: Women, from beginners to professionals
▶ Web site: ✍ *www.golfdigest.com/gfw*
▶ To subscribe: Call ✆ 1-800-374-7941

Here's an oasis for women in the middle of a male-dominated market. Like other golf magazines, there are articles and departments on instruction, equipment, and travel, but with a warmer tone. Fashion is focused on more here than in other golf magazines. Women's health is also different from men's, and *Golf for Women* addresses this, too.

Golf World

▶ Circulation: 150,000 +
▶ Written for: Golfers interested in national and international golf
▶ Published: Weekly, except for three times in November and once in December
▶ Web site: ✍ *www.golfdigest.com/newsandtour*
▶ To subscribe: Call ✆ 1-800-627-4438

Published by *Golf Digest, Golf World* covers amateur, collegiate, professional, and international tournaments. Every month there is an in-depth article on golf architecture. Also included are profiles of national and international pros on the various tours.

The Senior Golfer

▶ Circulation: (approx.) 150,000
▶ Published: Bimonthly
▶ To subscribe: Call ✆ 1-203-459-5190

This publication focuses on the senior market and its issues, covering equipment innovations, travel and leisure, fashion, and course designs. Instructional tips, along with profiles of senior players, are also included.

Appendix B

Glossary

A

ace: A hole in one; a hole completed in one stroke.

address: The position a player takes in preparing to strike the ball.

approach: Usually refers to the shot made to the green; also, the section of the fairway near the green (you'll probably never hear it used in this second context).

apron: The last several feet of fairway around the green.

away: As in "You're *away*," and meaning, it's your time to play because your ball is farthest from the hole. The person who is "away" always plays first between tee and green, and on the putting surface.

B

best ball: A match in which teams compete against the best score posted by a player on the other team on each hole. Each team posts its "best ball" (its best score) on each hole as the team score.

birdie: One stroke less than par on a hole; for example, a three on a par four.

blade: To hit the upper part of the ball by the edge of the club face, causing the ball to hug the ground in flight.

blind: As in "a blind shot"; usually refers to an approach from which the player striking the ball has no sight of the green.

bogey: One stroke over par on a hole; for example a five on a par four.

borrow: In putting, stroking the ball to the left or right of a straight line to the hole to compensate for the slope of the green.

brassie: Another name for a two wood.

break: The path a putt must follow over a contour in the green in order to go in the hole.

C

caddie: One who carries a golfer's clubs during play. Ordinarily well-versed in the game, knows the course, becomes a good judge of your game quickly, and will offer sound advice to make a round more enjoyable, and your score better.

carry: The distance traveled by a ball from where it was struck to where it first touches the ground. Used in a sentence: "That shot carried 265 yards." Also refers to clearing an obstacle, as in, "It's 265 yards to carry that bunker."

chip: A short approach shot in which the ball is struck with a lofted club so that it carries a desired distance (usually short) and runs (rolls) toward the pin. When the shot is executed from several dozen yards off of the green, the shot is called a pitch and run. The idea is the same: carry the ball over an obstacle, a bunker, a creek, a hill, or a slope, and let it run.

club face: The part of the club head that is supposed to hit the ball.

concede: Used in match play, to grant that an opponent has won a hole before play is completed on that hole; or, to grant that your opponent will sink (make) the next short putt, and allow him or her to pick up the ball rather than play the next putt.

course: The area in which play is permitted.

D

dead ball: A ball barely off of the hole, making the next putt an absolute certainty.

default: Concede a match without playing it.

divot: A slice of turf lifted by a club during a stroke. Golfing etiquette requires it must be replaced and pressed down.

dormie: In match play, describes the situation in which a team can't lose a match against the competition because the number of holes remaining is the same as the current lead. To go "dormie," means the player can't lose the match (at least in regulation).

down: The number of holes (in match play) or strokes (in medal play) a player is behind, as in "three down."

draw: A controlled and (slight) hook on the flight of the ball. Usually a draw rolls farther than a fade.

dub: A gentler term for a hacker; also to hit the ball poorly.

eagle: A score that's two strokes under par on a hole. A two on a par four (rare), a three on a par five (less rare). An ace (on a par three) is an eagle. A two on a par five is a double eagle.

face: The surface on the club designed to strike the ball; also, the steep slope of a bunker designed as part of the hazard.

fade: A shot that starts left of the target line and curves to the right toward the target line; not to be confused with a slice, which is unintentional.

fat shot: The club hits behind the ball, taking a divot before striking the ball. (See "thin shot" for comparison.)

featherie: Early golf balls with a core of compressed feathers inside a leather outer.

fore: A warning cry by a player to anyone along the flight path of the ball.

forecaddie: A caddie positioned ahead of the players to indicate the position of their shots as they come to rest.

four-ball match: A match in which one pair of players selects for their next shot the better positioned ball, against the better ball of a pair of opponents.

foursome: A group of four players; also, a match between two pairs in which each pair plays one ball.

G

groove: The indentations cut into the club face, which cause the ball to spin; also the description given to a good repeated swing.

ground: To place the head of the club on the ground to help you line up for the shot.

gutta-percha: Rubbery material used to make golf balls after 1848.

guttie: A golf ball made of gutta-percha, which rendered featheries obsolete.

H

halved hole: A hole played in the same number of strokes by opponents.

handicap: The number of stokes a player receives to equalize competition between otherwise unequal partners. Based on the lowest ten scores of the last fifteen scores recorded.

haskel: First incarnation of the modern golf balls with rubber straps wound around core.

heel: The part of the club head that is closest to you.

hole out: Make the final stroke that plays the ball into the hole. The last putt, usually; or the shot from off the green that finds its way into the hole.

honor: To drive off the next tee first, because of making the lowest score on the previous hole; the honor may not be declined.

hook: For a right-handed golfer, a stroke that caused the ball to curve to the left (the ball rotates counterclockwise).

hosel: The part of the club that attaches the club head to the shaft.

L

lie: The position of the ball on the ground (turf, behind a tree, in a bunker, and so on.); also (but less frequently) refers to the angle formed by the shaft and the club head.

links: A seaside golf course; or, a course laid out so that the first nine form a line out to the farthest point, and the last nine form a line beside the first holes coming back.

lip out: To get close to the rim of the cup but not make the hole.

loft: This term can be used in three ways. It can refer to the slant on the face of a club; the angle of the club face in relation to the ground; and the act of hitting the ball into the air, that is, to loft the ball.

lying: As in "lying three," meaning you have three penalty points.

M

mashie: Old-fashioned hickory-shafted iron, varieties of which were similar to today's five, six, and seven.

mulligan: A courtesy second tee shot after a bad shot. Usually granted to a player once during a round of golf; never used in competition.

N

Nassau: A scoring system under which one point is awarded for winning the first nine holes, a second point for winning the second nine, and a third point is awarded for the lowest score over the entire eighteen.

net: The score after the handicap strokes have been deducted.

niblick: Another name for a nine iron.

O

open: A tournament in which both professionals and amateurs are eligible to compete.

P

par: The number of strokes officially assigned to a hole or to the entire course. Par for a hole is determined by the number of strokes that should be necessary to reach the green plus two putts: a par three, one shot to the green plus two putts; a par four, two shots to reach the green and two putts. Par for the course is determined by the sum of par for each hole.

penalty: The number of strokes added to the score due to an infraction of the rules.

pin: The pole to which the flag is attached; the pole in the cup on each green.

pitch: A high, lofted approach shot.

pitch and run: A long chip.

pull: For a right-handed golfer, a shot that heads undesirably to the left on impact.

push: For a right-handed golfer, a shot that heads undesirably to the right on impact.

putt: A short stroke that makes the ball roll along the ground; usually (but not always) made on the green.

R

run: The distance a ball rolls after striking the ground.

S

slice: For a right-handed player, a stroke that sends the golf ball curving to the right of the intended line of flight.

shank: A ball struck with the hosel of the club (the part that attaches the club head to the shaft).

skull: To hit the ball with the blade of the club and send it scurrying much farther than desired. Fear of skulling the ball leads to deceleration, and even poorer shots that scoot wide to the right and left.

sole: The bottom of the club head; the part that rests on the ground.

square: Sometimes "all square;" a match that is even (tied).

stroke: Any forward motion of the club for the purpose of hitting the ball.

stroke hole: A hole on which a handicap stroke is given.

stymie: The situation caused when an opponent's ball lies in the direct line between the cup and another player's ball.

Surlyn: Tear-resistant plastic outer of modern golf balls (by DuPont Corp.)

T

takeaway: When the club head is moved back from the ball at the start of a swing.

Texas wedge: Name given to a putter when used anywhere other than the green.

thin shot: The club strikes the ball and never strikes the ground. (See "fat shot" for comparison.)

threesome: A group of three players; also, a match in which one player competes against two others, the two playing alternate strokes with the same ball.

toe: The part of the club head farthest from you.

top: To hit the ball above its center.

U

up: The number of holes (in match play) or the number of strokes (in medal play) a player is ahead.

W

worm burner: A shot that rolls along the ground.

Index

THE EVERYTHING YOGA BOOK

By Cynthia Worby, M.S.W., M.P.H., R.Y.T.

Are you experiencing added stress in your life? Feeling out of shape? *The Everything® Yoga Book* is the perfect introduction to this life-changing art form and physical regimen that has been practiced for more than 500 years. *The Everything® Yoga Book* shows you exactly how to get started—from basic poses that will make you feel great to special postures for particular ailments. It features simple relaxation and meditation techniques; soothing stretches; and specific suggestions for women, children, and seniors.

Trade paperback,
$14.95 ($22.95 CAN)
1-58062-594-0, 336 pages

OTHER *EVERYTHING®* BOOKS BY ADAMS MEDIA CORPORATION

BUSINESS

Everything® **Business Planning Book**
Everything® **Coaching & Mentoring Book**
Everything® **Home-Based Business Book**
Everything® **Leadership Book**
Everything® **Managing People Book**
Everything® **Network Marketing Book**
Everything® **Online Business Book**
Everything® **Project Management Book**
Everything® **Selling Book**
Everything® **Start Your Own Business Book**
Everything® **Time Management Book**

COMPUTERS

Everything® **Build Your Own Home Page Book**
Everything® **Computer Book**

Everything® **Internet Book**
Everything® **Microsoft® Word 2000 Book**

COOKING

Everything® **Bartender's Book, $9.95**
Everything® **Barbecue Cookbook**
Everything® **Chocolate Cookbook**
Everything® **Cookbook**
Everything® **Dessert Cookbook**
Everything® **Diabetes Cookbook**
Everything® **Low-Carb Cookbook**
Everything® **Low-Fat High-Flavor Cookbook**
Everything® **Mediterranean Cookbook**
Everything® **One-Pot Cookbook**
Everything® **Pasta Book**
Everything® **Quick Meals Cookbook**
Everything® **Slow Cooker Cookbook**

Everything® **Soup Cookbook**
Everything® **Thai Cookbook**
Everything® **Vegetarian Cookbook**
Everything® **Wine Book**

HEALTH

Everything® **Anti-Aging Book**
Everything® **Dieting Book**
Everything® **Herbal Remedies Book**
Everything® **Hypnosis Book**
Everything® **Menopause Book**
Everything® **Stress Management Book**
Everything® **Vitamins, Minerals, and Nutritional Supplements Book**
Everything® **Nutrition Book**

HISTORY

Everything® **American History Book**

All Everything® books are priced at $12.95 or $14.95, unless otherwise stated. Prices subject to change without notice.
Canadian prices range from $11.95–$22.95 and are subject to change without notice.